LOCOMOTION PAPERS   LP248

The Mansfield-Southwell-Rolleston Railway

by
Robert Western

© Oakwood Press & Robert Western 2021

Published by Oakwood Press, an imprint of Stenlake Publishing Ltd, 2021

British Library Cataloguing in Publication Data
A Record for this book is available from the British Library
ISBN 978 0 85361 757 0

Printed by Claro Print, Office 26, 27, 1 Spiersbridge Way, Thornliebank, Glasgow G46 8NG

All rights reserved. No part of this book may be reproduced or transmitted in any form or by any means, electronic or mechanical, including photocopying, recording or by any information storage and retrieval system, without permission from the Publisher in writing.

By the same author
The Ingleton Branch, Oakwood Press, 1990 (Revised Edition, 2018)
   (First published as *The Lowgill Branch*, Oakwood, 1971)
The Eden Valley Railway, Oakwood Press, 1997 (Revised Edition, 2014)
The Cockermouth Keswick and Penrith Railway, Oakwood Press, 2001
   (Revised Edition, 2007)
The Coniston Railway, Oakwood Press, 2007
The Kendal & Windermere Railway, Oakwood Press, 2012
The Mansfield Railway, Oakwood Press, 2019

Front cover: Johnson 0-4-4T No. 58056 on 'The Paddy' at Southwell on 19th April, 1952. The 16A shedplate relates to Nottingham but the engine was based at the sub-shed at Southwell. *Jack Cupit*

Title page: The Nottinghamshire coalfield was sometimes referred to as the land of the 2-8-0s and for good reason. Mansfield Colliery Junction is host to four of the type, no less, the nearest one being on the main line with coal from Rufford Colliery heading to Kirkby sidings, the pair with brake van ready to reverse down the branch to Crown Farm (Mansfield) Colliery and the furthest one just lurking with no apparent intent. *Jack Cupit*

Rear cover, top: Mansfield shed's long-time resident '4F' class No. 44416 heads a Southwell races special working at Mansfield Colliery Junction where the signalman is about to hand over the single line token to the crew. *Jack Cupit*

Rear cover, bottom: A 1923 Railway Clearing House map showing the Mansfield Southwell-Rolleston railway and its environs.

Oakwood Press, 54-58 Mill Square, Catrine, KA5 6RD
Tel: 01290 551122 *Website:* www.stenlake.co.uk

Contents

	Preamble	6
Chapter One	**The Act to build a railway, 1846-1864**	
	The Act to build a railway from Clay Cross via Mansfield and Southwell to Rolleston – The line opens between Southwell and Rolleston – Passenger services become spasmodic – Unrest in the locality	7
Chapter Two	**Another Act, 1865-1889**	
	Unrest in the local communities grows – A series of public meetings – The Midland changes its plans – A further Act – More unrest – The section from Southwell to Mansfield is built – Sand...	15
Chapter Three	**New prospects for the line, 1890-1929**	
	The demise of the Midland - the LMS – Passenger services withdrawn between Mansfield and Southwell – 'The Paddy' continues – Along the line	35
Chapter Four	**Further growth in the coalfield, 1930 to closure**	
	Oil – Nationalization – British Railways – Single servicing of collieries and further cut-backs – Closure east of Farnsfield – The nature trail – Closure west of Farnsfield – The end of the line	58
Chapter Five	**Motive power**	105
	Sources	111
	Acknowledgements and thanks	111
	Index...	112

'Peak' class No. 45051 crosses the viaduct over the River Maun with a brake van on the south-to-east curve having passed above Quarry Lane on 28th February, 1983. The floodlight tower in the distance marks the location of Field Mill, the home of Mansfield Town Football Club. *Malcolm Rush*

Midland Railway map of 1913.

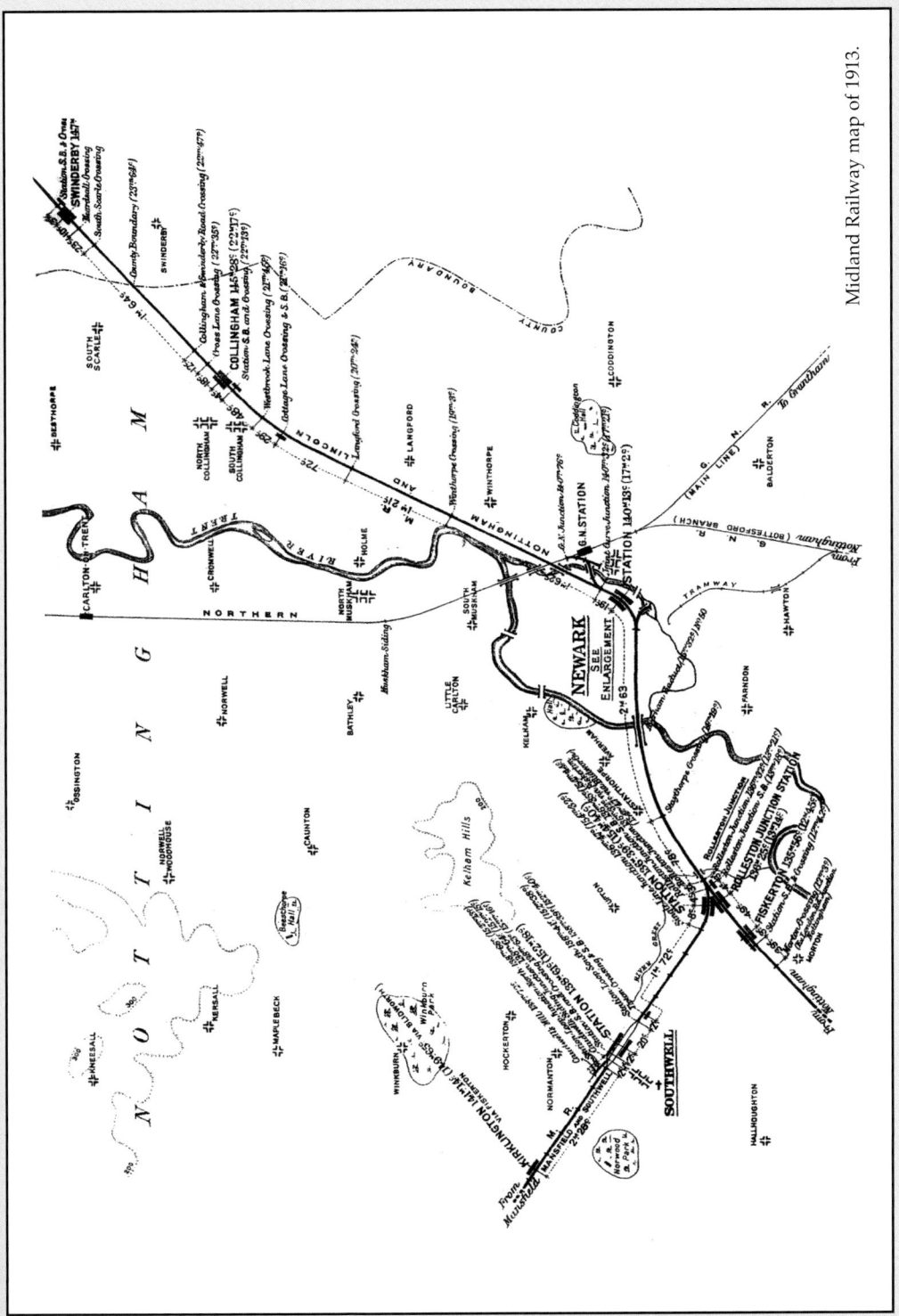

Midland Railway map of 1913.

Preamble

The Midland Railway (MR) was a highly ambitious and progressive company which was keen to ensure it would keep ahead of rivals. In some situations this was seen to be done by aggressive development in areas where there was possible competition likely. In the early days it could be (and sometimes was) argued that it had inherited some of the characteristics of George Hudson, the so-called 'Railway King' who had laid many of the foundations from which the Midland Railway had been built. Although he overreached himself and was subsequently 'dethroned' there were times shortly afterwards when mention was made in meetings held in connection with the Mansfield to Southwell line suggesting that his spirit could perhaps still be seen at work!*

The railway planned from Clay Cross (south of Chesterfield) to Mansfield, Southwell and Rolleston where it would meet the line from Nottingham to Lincoln via Newark became something of a battleground when the local communities felt the Midland seemed prepared to renege on its original plans for what many saw as less than acceptable reasons.

This giant, however, had not realised the measure of the dogged persistence of the people living in the area through which the proposed railway would pass, not least in the section between Southwell and Mansfield. With considerable tenacity they were quite ready to challenge the mighty Midland, if need be in Parliament, when the company appeared ready to abandon the promises it had made.

Nevertheless, completion was a long time coming and even when opened the line had something of a chequered history.

However, in its final years it did have a very important role to play which, if those who promoted it had lived to experience these matters, would have felt justified in getting the line built.

---

* The name George Hudson comes up quite regularly in the discussions during the early meetings in connection with the line between Southwell and Mansfield. George Hudson was a linen-draper living in York who, after being left a considerable sum of money when the railway system was in its infancy, was quick to see the financial rewards it could bring. He became involved with a number of projects at a time when these were, in effect, fragmented and just local schemes. His aggressive business stance made him enemies but he was able to bring small companies together to create stronger units. However, in his drive to do this he overstepped the law relating to financial practices and was eventually, in 1849, found guilty of malpractice and had to step down from the 'empire' he had created. For some his influence gave the Midland Railway, in its early days, something of a bad name for what appeared to be a 'left-over' of his aggressive stance.

[Further reading *The Railway King, A Study of George Hudson and the Business Morals of his Times*, by Richard S. Lambert (George Allen & Unwin, 1934).]

Chapter One

The Act to build a railway, 1846-1864

1846

On the 16th July, 1846 an Act Vict. cap. clvii was placed on the statute book and this gave authority to the Midland Railway 'to make a Railway from the Midland Railway at Clay Cross to join the Nottingham and Lincoln Railway with branches'. There may well have been those who saw this as offering a real benefit, certainly as far as Southwell was concerned. The canal era had passed it by, not being a centre which might have been seen to justify such a facility but the coming of the railway era was opening up new prospects. These were, not least, from the point of mobility and the easier acquisition of goods and provisions and also the added benefit of sending out the produce from this rural community, very much based on farming, availability of a wider market.

The decision was made whereby the first element in this project would be to build at the easterly end from Rolleston, which was on the line from Nottingham to Lincoln, and thence to Southwell (a distance of 2½ miles). This presented no problems and took only a short time to build.

Southwell Minster with its fascinating history, attracted excursions from as far afield as London soon after the railway opened. It has been said there was possibly a church on the site since 627 and after many changes, the present building, which became a cathedral in 1884, was and still is, a great attraction for visitors. *W. Taylor Collection*

ANNO NONO & DECIMO

VICTORIÆ REGINÆ.

∗∗

Cap. clvii.

An Act to empower the *Midland* Railway Company to make a Railway from the *Midland* Railway at *Clay Cross* to join the *Nottingham and Lincoln* Railway, with Branches.   [16th *July* 1846.]

WHEREAS an Act was passed in the Seventh and Eighth Years of the Reign of Her present Majesty, intituled *An* 7 & 8 Vict. *Act to consolidate the* North Midland, Midland Counties, c. 18. *and* Birmingham and Derby Junction *Railway Companies*, whereby certain Railways therein mentioned were vested in the *Midland* Railway Company under the Name of the *Midland* Railways : And whereas the making of a Railway from the *Midland* Railway near the *Clay Cross* Station thereon in the County of *Derby* to join the Line of the *Nottingham and Lincoln* Railway in the Parish of *Rolleston* and County of *Nottingham*, as authorized to be made by an Act passed in the last Session of Parliament, with Branches therefrom to *Sutton in Ashfield*, and to join the Line of the *Mansfield and Pinxton* Railway, and also the Line of a proposed Railway from *Nottingham* to *Mansfield*, would be attended with great local and public Advantage : And whereas the *Midland* Railway Company are willing to undertake the Execution of the said Railway and Branch Railways, if authorized by Parliament so to do : And whereas Two

[*Local.*]   33 *C*   Acts

The Railway Act of 16th July, 1846.

THE ACT TO BUILD A RAILWAY, 1846-1864

1847

On Thursday 1st July, 1847 the line between Rolleston and Southwell was opened. The *Nottingham Review & General Advertiser* noted this event and no doubt expecting more would follow headed the item 'Clay Cross and Newark Railway'.

> That part of the line which is completed up to Southwell from Rolleston was opened for traffic on the 1st inst. and many parties from Southwell availed themselves of a ride by steam on that day.

The *Leicestershire Mercury* also carried the story finishing with, 'It will be a very great accommodation'. In spite of this there seems to have been no great ceremony which often accompanied the opening of a railway in this period, however small. Perhaps it was decided to hold back until the railway was completed throughout and then there could be the usual junketing which often was the case for such an event. However, as will be seen, it would be a very long time before there would be the opportunity for that to take place.

From the account in the *Nottingham Review & General Advertiser* it would seem there was a good deal of enthusiasm to travel behind a steam locomotive. However, it was a passing experience. The Midland Railway timetables published shortly after the opening have no details about any services on the line.

Even in the month following the opening, in the Midland timetables for the line from Lincoln to Nottingham, and places beyond, it simply indicates that trains stop at 'Fiskerton for Southwell' and there is no mention of Rolleston at all. A considerable number of years later the timetables would indicate the means whereby passengers could be conveyed to Southwell from Fiskerton but for the time being the traveller to Southwell might well wonder how the journey could be completed.

In the years to come, there would be problems with a 'go-stop-go' situation as far as the Midland Railway policy about trains for Southwell was concerned and the outlook did not seem encouraging. Local dissatisfaction would grow and the Midland would come in for a lot of local criticism.

The fact that even this short section of the proposed line may not have come up to the possible expectation the Midland had hoped for, might well have led to misgivings by the company. Subsequently it seemed to become rather apprehensive and would even appear to question the wisdom about moving the project forward to achieve the original objective.

1848

However, in the meantime there were those who hoped to take advantage of this new facility. Messrs Stephenson & Co. of Clay Cross Collieries and Crich Lime Works provided items 'for farming communities'. Listed were 'Agricultural Crich Lime, both chemical and prepared, also hard and soft coals for a variety of uses' and several other items. Now that Southwell had a rail connection they were able in their advertisements in various newspapers to include it as one of the places where they could deliver these goods. This must have been seen as a possible boon for the local farmers. No doubt the farming communities which were situated along the proposed extension to the line such as Farnsfield and others, could expect to have this facility as well in the not too distant future. Possibly Stephenson & Co. could also see in this development the business potential because once the link to Clay Cross had been made, and if they were well established at Southwell and the immediate district, it could mean an expanding market for them. Unfortunately, if this was the case, they would be disappointed as well as the farmers in the outlying districts; the wait would be much longer than they may have anticipated.

Another potential impact which the new railway had, with its anticipated greater and easier access to other places, the like of which had not been available before, was in the sale or renting of property. Those placing advertisements in the newspapers were keen to point out the close proximity of a railway. The Revd J.C. Cunningham advertising in the *Derby Mercury* on 1st November, made a point of including when wishing to let a property in Southwell, that 'there is now a railway branch 2 miles in length with connections to Nottingham and Newark'.

However in spite of this, certainly for the latter aspiration, it was, for a short time at any rate, not to be the case.

1849

At the opening of the year there were trains running to Southwell. The service is rather spasmodic and the timetable which the Midland Railway issued lacks some clarity. Rolleston is not mentioned and the trains are linked with those between Lincoln, Nottingham and beyond. The essential pattern with those involving Southwell is as follows:

Weekdays only		*Class* 1st, 2nd, Parl. am	*Class* 1st, 2nd pm	*Class* 1st, 2nd pm	*Class* 1st, 2nd, 3rd pm
Lincoln	*dep.*	8.20	12.20	2.30	5.30
Newark		9.00	1.00	3.00	6.15
Southwell	*arr.*	9.50	1.45	3.40	6.55
Southwell	*dep.*	8.45	12.25	2.45	5.30
[intermediate stations to]					
Nottingham	*arr.*	10.00	1.50	3.45	7.05
[then on to Derby]					

Times from Southwell to Nottingham vary according to the number of stops en route.

Weekdays only		Class 1st, 2nd, 3rd am	Class 1st, 2nd pm	Class 1st, 2nd pm	Class 1st, 2nd pm
[From Derby]					
Nottingham	dep.	10.10	12.15	3.40	5.00
[intermediate stations to]					
Southwell	arr.	11.15	1.45	4.40	5.56
Southwell	dep.	10.30	12.25	3.50	
Lincoln	arr.	11.45	1.45	4.55	6.40

Parliamentary class, brought in by the government's Railway Regulation Act of 1844, required that all railway companies must provide at least one service each day in each direction and at a cheap rate in this category. There was considerable hostility to this law by some railway companies and in many cases the provision was very basic. Eventually, the Midland with its rather progressive outlook when it came to passenger services did provide in some cases twice that amount with better travelling conditions.

It will be seen in this case that as far as the journey from Lincoln is concerned there is just one train in this category but not one 'Parliamentary' train on the return trip from Nottingham. This is because a previous journey which commenced at Derby but terminated at Nottingham was a Parliamentary train and this presumably came within the regulations of 'at least one train in each direction'. It would seem this arrangement met the regulations although perhaps stretching them a little.

A service showing much the same pattern continued during the year but in September although Southwell is included on the timetable there is no service listed - there are just blank spaces! The Midland had seen fit to withdraw the facility for passengers in August and by November Southwell has been deleted altogether from the listings.

The 1850s

In the timetables issued early in 1850 Southwell is still omitted and this situation continued for several months. The timetables issued in August 1850 for the line which included Lincoln, Newark and Nottingham, once again did list Fiskerton for Southwell with no mention about the section of line for Southwell from Rolleston. It is not clear why the Midland had decided against reintroducing the service but presumably it had not been seen to be viable. It was felt in some quarters that the Midland did not seem to be demonstrating a great deal of enthusiasm for the support of this facility as far as the people of Southwell were concerned. This would become more prevalent as time went on. In April 1852 the Midland saw fit to reopen the line again but by March 1853 took the move of closing the line completely. There were clearly growing misgivings about this in the local community.

1860-1863

By the early part of 1860 the Midland had still suspended passenger traffic on the Southwell branch. On this occasion, when the line was closed to passenger traffic, the timetable did mention the introduction of an 'omnibus service' which was set up to connect with trains on the Nottingham-Lincoln line. At the time an omnibus usually signified a horse and fairly basic carriage.

The timetable again gives this connection as being 'at Fiskerton' and not all the trains on the Nottingham to Lincoln line had this facility to convey passengers to Southwell. The timetable lists omnibus connections at Fiskerton with these trains:

Trains to Nottingham	8.11 am*	11.03 am	4.56 pm*	
Trains from Nottingham	8.45 am*	11.55 am	4.20 pm	8.09 pm*

However, by January 1861 the Midland had decided to restore a service to Southwell and had issued a timetable. The information is very basic with no other stations listed.

		am	am	pm	pm
Nottingham	dep.	8.05	10.55	3.55	7.30
Southwell	arr.	9.00	11.45	4.55	8.25

		am	am	pm	
Southwell	dep.	7.55	10.55	4.35	
Nottingham	arr.	8.50	11.35	5.25	

Oddly no connections at Rolleston are listed. If these were, in fact, through trains there would have to be a reversal at Rolleston given at this stage and for many years afterwards the only junction at Rolleston was east facing.

Quite what had prompted this decision is not clear. Certainly there were growing misgivings in the local communities about the behaviour of the Midland and this would grow. These 'growing misgivings' really started to become more tangible towards the end of 1862.

On Saturday 28th December, 1861 a meeting was arranged in Mansfield. It was described as being held by 'the principal residents' and was at the Corn Exchange. Its purpose was 'to take into consideration the insufficient railway accommodation in Mansfield and the district'. Sir E.S. Walker, Bart, presided and a resolution was passed that 'the railway to and from Mansfield is insufficient and unsatisfactory'. A group was appointed which was made up of the Sir E.S. Walker, Major Salmond, Mr Hollins, Mr Watkin, Mr Getting and Mr Walker. The brief was 'to approach the Board of Directors of the Midland Railway with a view to them remedying their grievances'. There had been a letter from the Rt Hon. J.E. Denison, the Speaker of the House of Commons, who agreed to help them with their objectives. He pointed out that in his view 'Mr Beale the Chairman of the Midland Railway is an approachable person'.

Although the Mansfield to Southwell line was not named on this occasion it would soon become abundantly clear that this was one of their grievances with

---

* Parliamentary class.

the other being the line to Worksop. The whole issue would become a movement against the Midland Railway in view of what was seen as its apparent unwillingness to get on and finish building the railway that had been planned. Passenger services continued running during 1863 and these operated to the same timetable.

1864

It was soon realised by those with an eye to business that the coming of the railways could give a whole new meaning to the word 'Excursion'. This had been very much the preserve of the very wealthy and even then from the point of view of the travel element something not very comfortable and rather slow. The railways could change all this not least with those wanting to indulge in that notable Victorian pastime of 'improving the mind'. Here was the possibility to travel with comparative ease and visit places of interest. Southwell was such a place with its ancient church (not yet a cathedral) and a former Archbishop's Palace and, of course, Sherwood Forest nearby with its tales of Robin Hood. 'Marcus' in London realised this and amongst his rail excursions which were advertised in the London press, he listed Southwell.

For example on 9th July there was an advertisement for 'Marcus's Cheap Summer Excursions'. The prices from London Euston to Southwell were 8s. in closed carriages and 16s. in first class (in today's prices £49 and £98 respectively). The time of departure was 1.00 pm and clearly this excursion would run over a number of days but these were not given unless a potential customer acquired a leaflet. The use of the term 'closed carriages' was one frequently found at this time because some companies used open ones for the cheaper seats. Many of Marcus' excursions used the London & North Western Railway (LNWR) for some of the journey and then the Midland. The latter would be used for the part into Southwell.

During this year the Midland had been looking again at the original plan to build a line from Clay Cross to Southwell and beyond.

Clearly no further steps had been taken to make this a reality by extending the short section from Rolleston to Southwell and the Midland had decided that revision of the scheme was needed. As a result a Bill had been put before Parliament which would result in a new Act.

This would give rise to further misgivings within the local communities about the underlying motives the Midland might have in taking this action.

The sort of feelings expressed at the meeting in Mansfield in 1862 would begin to gain momentum as other groups joined in the action to get answers and some action by the Midland.

ANNO VICESIMO OCTAVO & VICESIMO NONO

VICTORIÆ REGINÆ.

Cap. ccclix.

An Act for enabling the *Midland* Railway Company to construct Railways from *Mansfield* to *Southwell*, and from *Mansfield* to *Worksop*, with a Branch to *Staveley*, and other Branches; and for other Purposes. [5th *July* 1865.]

WHEREAS it is expedient that the *Midland* Railway Company (in this Act called "the Company") should be empowered to construct Railways from *Mansfield* to *Southwell* and from *Mansfield* to *Worksop*, with a Branch to *Staveley* and other Branches: And whereas it is also expedient that the Company should be empowered to make certain Deviations in the *Nottingham and Mansfield* Line of their Railway: And whereas Plans and Sections showing the Lines and Levels of the proposed Railways and Works and the Lands which the Company are by this Act empowered to acquire for the Purposes thereof, and Books of Reference to such Plans containing the Names of the Owners or reputed Owners, Lessees or reputed Lessees, and Occupiers of the said Lands, have been deposited with the Clerks of the Peace for the Counties of *Nottingham* and *Derby* respectively: And whereas it is expedient that the Company should be empowered to raise a further Sum of

[*Local.*]   64 *S*   Money

The Railway Act of 5th July, 1865.

Chapter Two

Another Act, 1865-1889

Local communities begin to take the Midland to task. In July 1865, nearly 20 years after the previous Act of 1846, involving a line from Clay Cross to Mansfield and Southwell, the Midland made a new move. On 5th July, 1865 a further Act was placed on the statute book (28th & 29th Vict. cap. ccclix). The Midland clearly had had misgivings about the original proposal because the element involving Clay Cross had now been removed and by this latest Act, the Midland was enabled 'to construct Railways from Mansfield to Southwell and from Mansfield to Worksop with a branch to Staveley and other branches ...' In Section 19 of this Act is stated:

> No. 1 – A Railway to commence in the Parish of Mansfield in the County of Nottingham by a Junction with the Midland Railway and to terminate by a junction with the Midland Railway in the Parish of Southwell in the same County.

Clearly there continued to be some uneasiness locally about the way in which the Midland seemed to be dragging its heels over this project and this would manifest itself much more forcibly at a later date. There are two further sections in this Act which subsequently give rise to strong feelings. Section 18 states,

> All and every part of the Money to be raised under this Act whether by shares or borrowing shall be applied to the Purposes of this Act and to no other Purpose

Section 27 states,

> After the Expiration of the Period by this Act limited for the Completion of the Railways if the same be not then completed the Company shall be liable to a Penalty of Fifty Pounds *per* Day to be recoverable as a Debt due to the Crown for every day after the Period so limited until the same shall be completed and opened for Public Traffic......

A further section lists certain minor and unlikely exceptions to this. £50 a day would be a hefty price to pay in such circumstances and should have been a considerable incentive to get the line completed - but the Midland would come up with other plans which the people living in the locality, especially Southwell, would find completely unacceptable.

The delay of the Midland in getting on with the completion of the line was becoming a matter of considerable concern for those who felt the line should be built. Patience in some quarters was running out.

1867

With growing concern among the communities about the behaviour of the Midland it was felt the time had come for some form of action. The effort of the Mansfield Group had not appeared to have any real influence on the situation but it did seem to act as something of a catalyst to move the situation further. This resulted in a series of meetings centred mainly on Newark and Southwell.

On 9th February, 1867 one of the first of these was held in Newark. It is reported that it was a meeting 'of a very enthusiastic character' and given the parlance of the day this was probably a euphemism for something rather stronger. Attending 'was a host of leading bankers, solicitors, merchants and traders of the town'. Several resolutions were passed with all, in effect, urging the Midland to get on and complete the line by building the section from Southwell to Mansfield.

The previous day there had been a request by those organizing this meeting for 'the gentry and tradespeople' living in Southwell 'not wishing to lose so favourable an opportunity to draw a requisition'. As a result 115 did so and submitted the list for consideration by the Newark meeting.

In spite of the alleged enthusiasm of the Newark meeting, the outcome was a decision by a group in Southwell to call a further meeting. It was felt that the steps being taken were not sufficiently active enough and about 20 merchants and traders organized a meeting at the Crown Hotel in Southwell shortly afterwards. This meeting was 'well attended' and the Chairman on this occasion was Mr Jones. Those attending the meeting made it very clear that they wished to support the Newark Group and there is a sense here that momentum was gathering which would increase as time passed. A motion was proposed 'that it is important to the town of Southwell and the neighbouring villages that the railway from Newark [clearly demonstrating a wider brief] to Mansfield should be completed and that Newark and Southwell should combine in their endeavours'.

As was the wont on these occasions, 'Mr Seaton, spoke at considerable length.' During this he outlined the main reasons why there was the need to get the railway completed:

> To the rich as they could get to the north-eastern watering places more readily and cheaper.
> To the tradesmen whose goods would be delivered earlier.
> To the poor whose coal would be cheaper with the cost of carriage much less.

(Perhaps the priorities here are of interest.) He concluded by saying he felt 'the inhabitants had been trifled with by the Midland'.

There were other misgivings raised. For example, the fact that when going to Newark for the market on Wednesdays there were long waits at Rolleston and suggestions about how the Midland could better organize rail movements to make life easier for travellers from Southwell. It is very clear that a growing body of people was becoming uneasy about the Midland's intentions.

1868 – Meeting the Midland

At this point, in January, the press printed a very basic timetable for services between Southwell and Nottingham. There were no details for intermediate stations or of other connections.

Weekdays only		am	am	pm	pm	pm
Nottingham	*dep.*	8.00	11.10	1.43	3.45	7.50
Southwell	*arr.*	8.50	11.55	2.25	4.48	8.45
		am	am	pm	pm	
Southwell	*dep.*	7.40	11.00	1.40	4.12	
Nottingham	*arr.*	8.30	11.45	2.25	5.25	

The 3.45 pm included third class on Wednesdays and Saturdays.

With these continued growing concerns in the Southwell camp about the manner in which the Midland did not appear to be making any significant moves to complete the railway link with Mansfield, a suspicion began to grow that the delay suggested the Midland was 'up to something'. There then appeared to be some justification for this belief. News about a Midland meeting held on 15th January certainly did not seem to augur well.

This was a special meeting in Derby at which the Midland Directors informed the shareholders that there were considerable problems of a financial nature for the company, not least with rising costs which had not been anticipated on a number of schemes. In particular it involved the one associated with building the line to London. In short the Directors had decided on steps which they felt were necessary given the present circumstances and therefore wished to put to the shareholders a resolution. This, in brief, would involve the company either delaying or possibly abandoning any project that had not already been started. In addition to this proposal a further resolution was proposed asking Parliament for extensions of time for some projects already underway. After much discussion the shareholders voted almost unanimously to support the Directors on both these counts.

When news of this action by the Midland came to the notice of the communities in Newark, Mansfield and Southwell in particular, it was clearly seen as a warning sign and as a threat that the Southwell to Mansfield scheme would number among those about to be abandoned. This further fired up the attitudes of those living in these places.

On Saturday 1st February a meeting was convened at the Assembly Rooms in Southwell. Clearly the momentum for action was growing. It was stated that the purpose was 'to compel the Midland Railway to fulfil their commitments in relation to the Act of 1865'. There was a great deal of heated discussion and it was made very clear that the meeting had been convened following the decision made by the Midland Board and shareholders on 15th January. This was perceived as a situation which needed to be addressed.

On this occasion R. Millward was appointed the Chairman and he read a letter of support for their action from Mr Hodgkinson MP. The Chairman went on to explain the apparent lack of concern for those travelling to Southwell and provided information on the procedures he was criticizing. He pointed out that on numerous occasions there has been considerable inconvenience caused because trains had been stranded at Rolleston by being put in a 'side-way' (his term for 'siding'). 'Waiting times have been up to three-quarters of an hour whilst there would be ample time to bring them in to Southwell and back once or twice for the other train coming from Newark'. He went on to say that he wrote to James Allport about this and was at least heard because Allport replied, 'I have given instructions for the first train to run especially to Southwell and return at once for the second'.

The general feeling of the meeting was that the area needed and wanted 'direct communication with Mansfield' and this to be provided by the proposed railway. There were suggestions by the Chairman that the Midland was not a company to be trusted and claimed he had had first-hand experience of this when he was involved in a project for the 'Boston, Newark and Sheffield Railway' which would have linked with the Midland 'Sheffield, Liverpool and Manchester Railway'. He claimed that although it was the Duke of Devonshire who, on the face of it, was responsible for having the Bill defeated in Parliament it was, in fact, the Midland that was really the driving force in getting it thrown out. He had then gone to meet George Hudson who had proposed a deal whereby because any similar scheme would not be likely to be undertaken by another company, the Midland would be ready to undertake one which was similar. However, this never happened. This was just the sort of stuff the meeting seemed to want to hear and there were shouts, we are told, of 'Disgraceful' from some of those present. Another speaker remarks on the 'foolish' and 'rash' plan proposed by the Midland to build a line from Settle to Carlisle and there would be more to come on that subject later. After a lengthy meeting, a proposal was made to resist in whatever way possible, any attempt by the Midland to get out of the commitment to build the line from Southwell to Mansfield. More was to follow.

On 8th February another meeting was convened this time at the town hall in Newark. It was reported as being 'extremely well attended'. Feelings were now clearly running very high and some strong opinions were voiced. It had been hoped that Mr Hodgkinson MP would attend but he chose to send a letter instead. In it he made it clear that 'three or four years' previously he had taken an active part in negotiations with the Midland Railway which had resulted in the present Act (for its line) and recently he had been able to confer with 'gentlemen who were well up in the Councils of the Midland Railway'. He maintained that the Midland recognised the commitment made to build the line. In fact there had been a complaint on their part that there had been no attempt to communicate with them to ascertain this. However, in spite of this he did feel it was important to propose a resolution that it was of the utmost importance that the line should be built.

There were clearly some 'heavyweights' backing the meeting and they included several MPs and again including the Rt Hon. J.E. Denison, the Speaker of the House of Commons, who, it will be recalled, had been in contact with the Mansfield group six years before. Living as he did near Newark he continued to be much in favour of the proposals which were aired in the meeting. He did comment it was important to ascertain whether or not at that Midland meeting of 15th January at which there was a resolution of abandoning some schemes, the Southwell to Mansfield line had been included.

There were cheers at the meeting when they heard this but the following discussions still questioned the motives of the Midland's Directors. The point was made that a company which had £35,000,000 could surely afford to pay £70,000 to £80,000 to build their line.

The outcome was that on 21st February, a group from Southwell headed by Mr Millward of Thurgaton Priory met with the Midland Board of Directors at what was described as 'a special meeting'. Mr Millward was joined by Mr Nicholson, representing Newark, Mr Stenton for Southwell and Mr Maude for Mansfield. The Southwell group opened the meeting by outlining their objective in attending. They explained their grievances about the delay to the project. Hutchinson, Chairman of the Midland replied that he regretted there were such grievances and said that his company did not intend to abandon the line but it planned to ask Parliament for an extension of time. Stenton expressed great regret about this and said he felt Parliament would oppose any proposal to postpone and the others in the group agreed. In conclusion, after further discussion, the local group emphasized to the Board the extent of the hardship that would ensue if the line was not built.

Shortly afterwards, and it would seem and without any further discussion, the Midland promptly took the step of applying to Parliament for extensions ranging over a number of projects and schemes. These included the line from Mansfield to Southwell.

With several months having now passed and with still little apparent evidence of any progress by the Midland, there was what was described as 'another large important meeting' held on 23rd December in Southwell. This would prove not only to be important but full of ire which would be directed towards the Midland Railway Company. There would be strong words and a number of allegations.

It was reported that nearly all the trade and business people were represented together with many others. The Chairman, Mr Stenton (some reports say 'Steaton'), pointed out that they must now exert themselves or they would never obtain the line. They had a most powerful opponent (he said he was sorry to be obliged to use the word) to contend with. He did point out that he had expressed the wish that when they met it might be at a celebration dinner for the opening of the railway and went on to say that he *wished* [*sic*] it - he had not said he *hoped* it or even *expected* it because he 'expected nothing but ill-treatment and humbuggery from the Midland Railway Company'. He said that he 'had watched the company's proceedings for the line for twenty-five years and all he had observed was that the company used the district and abused it'.

Having said all this, he stressed that he felt the time had now come when long speeches were no longer necessary and went on to refer to other meetings which had already taken place particularly in Newark 'some months ago'. 'But' he stated, 'speeches were now over!' It was time for action.

There were further points made with one important one being that it was felt the Midland was determined to 'break the bond which Parliament had bound'. It was also pointed out that 25 years ago the Midland had given notice of the intention to build the line but any requests for extensions (it was alleged) were simply a ploy to get out of building it. It was agreed that now was the time to petition Parliament to reject a current Bill put forward by the Midland requesting a further delay. There was a great deal of debate and feelings seem to have been running high. Eventually there was a resolution put forward,

> That this meeting has heard with astonishment and regret that notwithstanding the Midland Railway Company's Acts of 1846 and 1865 and notwithstanding that the company is perfectly solvent with its stock at a considerable premium and paying a

large dividend has given formal notice of its intention to apply to Parliament for power to extend for the construction of the Railway from Southwell to Mansfield.

Reference was made to a number of Midland projects which the company appeared to have 'bought off'. There was then a second resolution which included the support of local villages. Support was given by W.P. Barrow MP and he pointed out a significant element, namely that the Midland had already called up the money authorized by Parliament in order to build the line and this factor would no doubt be the cause of considerable stress in some quarters. Once again, the Midland was clearly being seen in a very bad light.

Messrs Stenton, Gee and Hunter were appointed to prepare the petition. They were also asked to communicate with similar committees in Newark, Mansfield and Worksop.

The committee drew up a, very lengthy, petition. The preamble begins,

> To the honourable Commons of the United Kingdom of Great Britain and Ireland in Parliament assembled. The humble petition of the inhabitants of Southwell, Farnsfield, Halam, Edingley, Bilsthorpe, Kirklington, Winkbourne (Winkburn), Hockerton, Upton, Oxton and Halloughton ...

It noted,

> ... that in or about the year 1844 a company was formed for the purpose of making a railway from Boston to Sheffield passing through the towns of Newark, Southwell and Mansfield and that before an Act of Parliament was obtained The Midland Railway Company made proposals to that company which were ultimately accepted by which The Midland Railway Company undertook to make a line from Newark to Mansfield through to Southwell and in the year 1846 obtained an Act to carry out the arrangements.

It also pointed out that so far the only section that had been built was that from Rolleston to Southwell.

The second section, again lengthy, points to some of the history of the project and the Midland's behaviour in its dealings with the Great Northern Railway and the subsequent decision by the MR to build the line:

> In 1864 a company was formed for the purpose of making a line from the Great Northern Railway at Newark through the towns of Southwell and Mansfield to Staveley and applied to Parliament for the necessary powers. That again the Midland Railway stepped in and arrangements were entered into whereby the Midland Railway undertook – on the new company withdrawing - to obtain another Act to finish the undertaking defined by the Act of 1846 - that is to say to carry on the line from Southwell to Mansfield.

There would be those who read into this situation that the Midland's main objective in making this so called 'arrangement' was simply to block another company moving onto its territory and appeared in the long term to have no real intention of ever building the line.

The third section deals with the Midland's Act of 1865 and points out that five years were given for the building of the line. It goes on to point out that given the nature of the terrain through which the line would pass, this period was more than enough to complete it.

The fourth section raises an issue which was felt to be of a most important nature. It refers back to clause 18 in the Act, mentioned earlier, about the financial conditions. There is perhaps a hint in the wording here that the money which the Midland has already taken might have been used for other purposes even though the Act in question plainly stated that it could only be used for the railway proposed in the Act. (Shades here of George Hudson?) Clause 27 also referred to earlier, related to the penalty of £50 per day due to the Crown after the expiration of the time that the railway should be completed.

The fifth section simply takes a swipe at the Midland and suggests, in effect, that since the Act of 1846 the Midland had built lines not even contemplated in 1846 and which have enhanced the places where they have been built by bringing prosperity whilst the places that might have been served by their line have suffered poverty through being depressed. The implication was that in view of this the line from Southwell to Mansfield is considered to be a great necessity. There was some tough talking here and one or two inferences which possibly raised a few eye-brows in the Midland camp.

1869 – Building the Mansfield line at last

By the middle of January it was reported that the petition was ready for signatures and all were urged to sign. However, before this had happened there had been yet another meeting in Mansfield. Clearly the communities were not going to give up on the fight to get this railway built.

Once again the meeting was held at the Corn Exchange with a large number turning out which consisted mainly of tradespeople and farmers. The Mansfield group had two axes to grind. Not only was the Mansfield to Southwell line on the agenda but also the one from Mansfield to Worksop.

Once again the resolution was to petition Parliament to refuse to allow the Midland to default on taking action as set out in the Act and 'to keep faith with the Public by constructing to build railways to Worksop and Southwell according to the Mansfield Lines Act of 1865'.

The remark by Chairman Mr William Hollins of the Pleasley Works must have rung true with his listeners. He commented that they had had trouble enough already to induce the company to proceed. Once again the matter of the Midland's behaviour relating to the Great Northern came as he pointed out: 'The Great Northern would have been pleased to make it years ago but the Midland slipped in and prevented them'. It is reported 'Astonishment and indignation' was voiced in the drawing up of yet another resolution and yet again the opinion was aired that the impression was that the Midland would not build.

It eventually became clear that in spite of the petitioning the Midland had been working away in the background. On 12th July, an Act, namely Local Act 32, 33 Vict. cap. lxxxiii (Additional Powers) was introduced. The purpose of this,

> ... was for conferring additional powers on the Midland Railway Company for the construction of new works; for extending the periods for the purchase of certain lands, and the construction of certain authorized Railways and for other purposes.

[32 & 33 Vict.]   *The Midland Railway*   [**Ch. lxxxiii.**]
             (Additional Powers) Act, 1869.

CHAP. lxxxiii.

An Act for conferring additional powers on the Midland   A.D. 1869.
Railway Company for the construction of new works; for
extending the periods for the purchase of certain lands, and
for the construction of certain authorized Railways; and
for other purposes.   [12th July 1869.]

WHEREAS it is expedient that the Midland Railway Company (herein-after called "the Company") should be empowered to construct a short curve to connect their Leicester and Hitchin Line with the South Leicestershire Railway:

And whereas plans and sections showing the line and levels of the railway by this Act authorized to be constructed, and the lands by this Act authorized to be acquired, with a book of reference to such plans, have been deposited with the clerk of the peace for the county of Leicester, which plans and sections and book of reference are in this Act referred to as the deposited plans, sections, and book of reference:

And whereas it is expedient that the powers conferred upon the Company by the Midland Railway (Bristol Line) Act, 1863, (herein-after referred to as "the Bristol Line Act, 1863",) for the purchase of lands for the purposes of the railway thereby authorized should be revived:

And whereas it is expedient that the time limited by the Midland Railway (Chesterfield to Sheffield) Act, 1864, for the construction of the railway and works by that Act authorized should be extended:

And whereas it is expedient that the time limited by the Midland Railway (Bath and Thornbury Lines) Act, 1864, for the construction of the railways and works by that Act authorized should be extended:

And whereas it is expedient that the time limited by the Midland Railway (Mansfield, &c. Lines) Act, 1865, for the construction of the railways and works by that Act authorized should be extended:

[*Local.*—*83.*]   A   1

The Railway Act of 12th July, 1869. Note the reference to the Mansfield Act of 1865.

ANOTHER ACT, 1865-1889

A half-yearly meeting of the Midland took place on Wednesday 18th August. There was much on the agenda with a considerable number of railway projects to consider following the Act. The meeting was informed that the good news was that traffic receipts were up but the particularly bad news was that in spite of a deal being struck with the London & North Western Railway involving Scottish traffic over the Ingleton branch and a subsequent move to have the Act for the building of its own line between Settle and Carlisle rescinded, the Government had decided the Act must stand. This would cost the company dearly. However, the company had been granted a year's extension in the Parliamentary session for various projects and these included building the line from Southwell to Mansfield.

The meeting was further informed that Eckersley & Bayliss had been appointed the contractors on what were considered 'satisfactory terms' and the construction of the iron bridges was put in the hands of Handyside & Co. from Derby. The news that the extension time had been granted for the completion of the line may not have been to everybody's liking but fears that the line might never be built at all could be laid to rest. There may well have been relief in some sense and perhaps, at least, that, in part, the battle had been won and the Midland had been brought to book by the local communities. The railway between Southwell and Mansfield would be built.

The Midland dilemma

Reference, with a certain amount of derision, was made at the meetings in Southwell and Newark to the plan by the Midland to build a line from Settle to Carlisle. Whilst all the wrangling about building the line from Mansfield to Southwell had been going on, the Midland had been involved in another scheme and one which it certainly would have seen as having a much higher priority.

The Midland had been very keen and saw it as a high priority, to extend its influence north and into Scotland. However, it was finding it difficult to do this. Eventually it picked up what had been an abandoned project by 'The Little North Western' and this enabled it to open a line as far as Ingleton. At this point it met head-on with the London & North Western Railway's territory which was a continuance of this line from Ingleton to Lowgill where there was a link to the West Coast main line. Discussions between the Midland and the LNWR started as early as 1861 and the Midland tried in vain to strike a working arrangement with the LNWR whereby it would have been able, by passing over the rest of this branch, to reach the West Coast main line at Lowgill and thence to Carlisle and on to Scotland. The LNWR, not wanting its territory invaded by a possible rival, was perverse and its conditions relating to running powers were eventually unacceptable to the Midland. In 1866, after much wrangling and in what may have been seen as a last resort, the Midland instructed its engineer Crossley to set out a separate route from Settle and over the moorlands to Carlisle. Building such a line would be very expensive and this may well have led the Midland to be cautious about spending capital on what it probably saw as comparatively small and less important schemes such as the Mansfield to Southwell.

The Act to build a line from Settle to Carlisle was placed on the statute book in 1866. However, the LNWR now became convinced the Midland Act could lead to an even more damaging situation for its company. After intervention in 1868 by Richard Moon, the redoubtable Chairman of the LNWR, an acceptable deal was struck with the Midland. The Midland seized on this as it would be let off the hook as far as a very expensive project was concerned. This, in turn, at this stage, possibly relaxed the Midland's attitude to what were perceived as minor schemes elsewhere. But here was the irony, the Midland needed the Government to repeal the Settle & Carlisle Act if it was to abandon building the line. After a lengthy session from 8th to the 16th April, 1869, Parliament refused to do so, landing the Midland with the prospect of a project with a very large bill that it could well do without.

By this time the Bill with the plans for the extensions on construction times and other aspects relating to the making of the Southwell Railway (and other matters) was well advanced in going through Parliament. As stated earlier it became an Act on 12th July and there could really be no going back as far as that was concerned either!

By September work on building what had been decided would be a single track line with some passing loops was well underway. As was usually the case when a railway was built, a great influx of navvies appeared in the locality. On 11th September, W.E. Goodacre, who was the clerk to the guardians of a local poor house, wrote a letter to them and in it points out,

> Since the construction of a branch line of the railway from Southwell to Mansfield has started it has caused an influx of navvies and labourers who take up all available lodgings.

Clearly this was causing something of a problem as far as the availability of accommodation was concerned.

1870

At a meeting of the Midland Board in April, the only comment made about the Mansfield to Southwell project was that the work on the line was progressing in a satisfactory manner and about one-third of it was complete. The terrain through which the line was built is not particularly challenging, as had been pointed out on a number of occasions at the various meetings which had been held. However, there were sections in which hard sandstone was encountered and this was particularly so in two of the cuttings which had to be opened up near Rainworth. One of these was 32 ft deep and the other 28 ft deep. This section of the work required the use of gunpowder for blasting purposes and a considerable quantity was needed; it seems about 120 tons. This was risky stuff to use and at least two men were killed using it when blasting was carried out in these deep cuttings near Rainworth. It was a scenario sometimes encountered when using this material. The hole was drilled, the charge was placed in the hole, the fuse was lit, all retreated to a safe distance but an explosion did not occur after the period of time expected. While seeking to find the problem, an explosion subsequently did occur and on each of two occasions a workman was killed.

1871 – The lines open

By February the line had been completed and was ready for inspection. This was carried out on Wednesday 22nd February by Col C.S. Hutchinson, a Government Inspector. He was accompanied in this task by a group of people which included Mr Needham, superintendent of the Midland, Mr Barlow the consulting engineer, Mr Bayliss and Mr Terry, the engineers for the contractors, Mr Carr, the resident engineer, Mr Warwick, chief of the Telegraphic Department, Mr Prince together with others.

The inspection started at the Southwell end of the line. Included amongst the equipment for the inspection were two locomotives. The type was not specified in the report but it was said they were about 70 tons each.

The points and signals at the junction were tested first and then the members of the group moved on. They walked the five miles as far as Farnsfield examining the bridges, culverts and signals and then paused for a break and refreshment. After this they continued to Rainworth. An observer noted the 'splendid specimens of workmanship'. There was some conversation with some of the navvies at this point who informed the group that there had been pheasants which had been killed when they flew into the telegraph wires. Somewhat tongue in cheek, it seems, the navvies had said that they managed to deal with them.

So on to Mansfield and the 66 ft girder bridge en route over Southwell Road was given a thorough testing by the locomotives which were run backwards and forwards at full speed and then at slower speeds. The deflection was so slight that the inspector is recorded as saying 'The bridge stood like a rock'. It was also noted that the viaducts near Mansfield were of 'a very neat and substantial form and that the workmanship is of a most solid and durable kind'.

The inspector expressed satisfaction and the company was informed that after some minor adjustments to certain signals and points the railway could be opened on 1st March. It was fully opened for traffic on 3rd April. So the local people through determination and sheer perseverance had brought about the result for which they fought so hard.

Yet who would be right in the long run? Would the line be sustainable, as those who had made such an effort to have it built had felt or would the Midland in some sense be vindicated with the belief that the line would not really be viable? Time would tell and situations would occur that might give rise to a few surprises.

In the direction from the Nottingham-Lincoln line the first station was Rolleston (Junction). This had platforms on the Nottingham-Lincoln line and also the Southwell branch. The next was Southwell which also had an engine shed and a comparatively substantial goods yard together with a coaling plant. There were three intermediate stations along the line. After Southwell then came a station situated between Kirklington and Edingley both being about a mile from the line in a generally north and south direction respectively. The next station was Farnsfield where there was a goods warehouse and sidings. The final station before Mansfield was at Rainworth.

In the years when passenger services were operated, the Midland seemed to be uncertain about how the stations should be named. Southwell and also

THE MANSFIELD-SOUTHWELL-ROLLESTON RAILWAY

With the construction of the railway to Southwell a triangle of lines was formed to the south of Mansfield's Midland Railway station. These two *circa* 1875 views show the viaduct at Quarry Lane which carried the railway over the River Maun between Mansfield South Junction and Mansfield East Junction. *(Both) W. Taylor Collection*

This *circa* 1875 view shows the viaduct (now demolished) which also crossed Quarry Lane that carried the railway over the river between Mansfield North Junction and Mansfield East Junction. *W. Taylor Collection*

The bridge which carried the railway to Southwell over Nottingham Road looking towards Mansfield. This bridge was just to the east of Mansfield East Junction. *W. Taylor Collection*

The railway bridge over the Mansfield-Newark turnpike road (now Southwell Road, Mansfield) *circa* 1875. Note the windmill at Carter Lane in the distance. *W. Taylor Collection*

Blidworth station building *circa* 1875. *W. Taylor Collection*

Farnsfield retained these names throughout. However, the station near Edingley and Kirklington for which initially both names were used, later became just Kirklington. The station at Rainworth was referred to initially as Rainworth and then Blidworth. Ultimately it became known as Blidworth & Rainworth. In spite of this there are documents in this last period when 'Blidworth' was still being used. These changes in the names were reflected in the timetables.

With the line open it was necessary to dispose of various items which were no longer needed. An advertisement appeared in the *Derbyshire Courier* on Saturday 4th March. This was to the effect that J.E. Burrows had received instructions 'from Mr Cornish, the subcontractor on the Mansfield and Southwell Railway to offer on Friday next 10 March for sale in Mansfield Market the whole of the horses, carts' and a variety of other items. There were just four horses for sale. These were a bay horse 'Jewel' (10 years old) a brown horse 'Captain' (nine years old) a grey horse 'Punch' (six years old) and a bay mare 'Kit' - a half breed (five years old). It is stated that the horses were active and in good condition. Horses were used extensively in railway construction in this period and there are accounts about how harshly, indeed cruelly, they were often treated when some lines were being built. Perhaps the fact these horses were given names might suggest that in this situation they were better treated than was quite often the case elsewhere.

It seems apparent that the Midland felt there would never be a heavy demand for passenger services on the line and this is very clear from the timetables. Through trains from Lincoln and through Newark to Mansfield used the line.

During the period when passenger services were run, as mentioned previously, there was no west-facing junction at Rolleston and so there could be no through trains on the Southwell line from Nottingham to Mansfield. Given that there were good facilities along the other Midland line from Nottingham to Mansfield this is, perhaps, not surprising. For those in the villages along the Southwell line wanting to get to and from Nottingham it would be a matter of travelling to Rolleston and making a connection there as this would probably be more preferable than travelling to Mansfield and making the connection there. Connecting trains for this service were relatively convenient as far as waiting times were concerned.

1877

One group which was quick to see the benefits of this new railway facility was what eventually became known as the Mansfield Sand Co. Mansfield sand had been quarried on a commercial scale for some years by this time. The sand had a quality which made it particularly suitable for casting. As a result it was much sought after by foundries operating in the area and in places further afield such as Sheffield. It was also said that the sand had a superior quality to that which was being imported. In the edition of the *Sheffield Independent* on 16th October, 1877, the Berry Hill Sand Co. placed a notice inviting contractors to tender for the work of making a railway siding to the quarry on what was known at the time as the Berry

Farnsfield station *circa* 1875, view looking west towards Mansfield.　　W. Taylor Collection

Kirklington station *circa* 1875, view looking east towards Rolleston.　　W. Taylor Collection

Hill Estate. This branch would connect to the Mansfield-Southwell line. There was also another quarry between Berry Hill Road and Forest Road just to the west of the one on the Berry Hill Estate. The latter eventually set up its own internal mineral railway to link up with the main line of the railway and for many years a Manning, Wardle 0-4-0ST was used there to marshal wagons ready for dispatch. It had its own engine shed and was given the name *Empress*. It was still operating into the 1950s.

1878

By January 1878 the timetable was as follows:

Weekdays only		1st, 2nd, Parl.	1st, 2nd, Parl.	1st, 2nd, Parl.
		am	am	pm
Mansfield	dep.	6.15	9.35	3.40
Blidworth		6.32	9.48	3.52
Farnsfield		6.48	9.58	4.01
Kirklington		7.01	10.06	4.08
Southwell	dep.	7.30	10.13	4.14
Rolleston	arr.	7.38	10.21	4.23
Rolleston	dep.	7.47	10.44	4.28
Nottingham	arr.	8.30	11.28	5.10
Rolleston	dep.	7.45	10.22	4.27
Newark	arr.	7.55	10.30	4.35
Lincoln	arr.	9.30	12.38	5.43

Weekdays only		1st, 2nd, Parl.	1st, 2nd, Parl.	1st, 2nd, Parl.	1st, 2nd, Parl.
		am	am	am	pm
			ThO	ThX	
Lincoln	dep.	7.00	10.00	10.00	3.40
Newark	dep.	8.35	11.00	12.00	5.00
Rolleston	arr.	8.43	11.10	12.10	5.08
Nottingham	dep.	8.05	–	11.15	4.15
Rolleston	arr.	8.42	–	11.54	4.54
Rolleston	dep.	8.45	11.15	12.15	5.12
Southwell		8.51	11.26	12.33	5.18
Kirklington		8.58	11.32	12.43	5.25
Farnsfield		9.04	11.47	1.30	5.32
Blidworth		9.12	11.55	1.45	5.40
Mansfield		9.25	12.20	2.12	5.55

ThO – Thursdays only, ThX – Thursdays excepted.

On journeys to and from Nottingham to destinations to and from those on the Southwell line there are convenient connections at Rolleston. It can also be seen that the Midland is providing Parliamentary fares on all trains and this exceeds the statutory requirement.

The 1880s

There were very few mishaps on the line and no serious ones but at a time when these events did occur they were of interest to the press of the day because it was felt railway matters caught the attention of their readers. A member of staff for the *Mansfield Reporter* recorded an incident concerning the locomotive that would be taking a train from Mansfield along the line.

> As the locomotive was being brought out of the shed one of the springs broke and so the locomotive could not take the train out. A shunting engine was taken from the goods yard and attached to the train which after some delay set off. At Blidworth Station [the correct title at this juncture] the driver realised that the bearings had become 'overheated' and it is reported that 'the matter took time rectifying the problem'.

Clearly this was seen as news!

The timetable for 1889 carried very much the same structure as the one for 1878 but the connection facilities at Rolleston for trains to and from Nottingham are now omitted. In addition there seems to be more acknowledgement of passenger needs in terms of a market train being noted.

Weekdays only			ThO	ThX
	am	am	pm	pm
Mansfield	6.10	9.45	3.25	3.45
Blidworth	6.27	9.55	3.37	3.56
Farnsfield	6.54	10.02	3.45	4.04
Kirklington & Edingley	7.11	10.08	3.52	4.11
Southwell	7.25	10.14	4.00	4.20
Rolleston	7.32	10.20	4.07	4.27
Newark	7.43	10.30	4.15	4.35
Lincoln	9.10		5.55	5.55

Weekdays only	SO	ThO	MWFO	TuSO	
	am	am	am	am	pm
Lincoln	7.00	9.45		11.00	3.25
Newark	8.23	11.00	12.00	12.00	5.05
Rolleston	8.32	11.10	12.11	12.11	5.13
Southwell	8.37	11.23	12.22	12.22	5.19
Kirklington & Edingley	8.45	11.32	12.40	12.40	5.25
Farnsfield	8.51	11.41	1.00	1.20	5.31
Blidworth	8.58	11.50	1.07	1.48	5.38
Mansfield	9.09	12.05	1.20	2.05	5.50

MWFO – Monday, Wednesday and Friday only, TuSO – Tuesday and Saturday only, ThO – Thursdays only, ThX – Thursdays excepted, SO – Saturdays only.

Rainworth station is still being called 'Blidworth' (since 1877). It would become 'Blidworth and Rainworth' in 1894. It will be seen that the 6.10 am from Mansfield takes considerably longer to reach Rolleston than later trains. One possible explanation for this is that at this stage, like other lines of this type, the early train carried such things as newspapers, possibly mail and other items and time was allowed for the purpose of unloading these. The delay is greatest at Farnsfield the only place where there was a warehouse and this might explain why this is also the case. Presumably the times given are the departure times - essentially the only ones of interest to those catching the train.

Into the 1890s

In 1890 the timetable remains much the same although with just 'Thursday only/Thursday excepted variations. A notable change is that the 7.00 am from Lincoln runs through to Ambergate, arriving 10.34 am. There is no through return service listed on this timetable.

It has already been noted that the railway companies, including the Midland, very quickly saw the financial opportunities that excursions could present and the scope of such became very broad. One aspect of this which the Midland developed early in the Nottinghamshire area was the race and hunt meetings at Southwell. Without doubt a good many people would consider that one aspect of the line which was important was the operation involving the specials which were run in connection with these race meetings in Southwell.

The history of the Southwell racecourse spans over many years and meetings were being held long before the advent of the railway. Until 1898 the races were held in Southwell itself. The meetings were extremely popular and the Midland soon realised they could capitalize on this popular event. 'Cook's Fast Excursions' organized a considerable number of trips to the races over the years and this company worked with the Midland until its demise and then, its successor the London Midland & Scottish Railway (LMS). These excursions brought large numbers of people into Southwell who came from a variety of places with some being considerable distances away. Tamworth is a place listed frequently as a starting point in the advertisements. In addition the Great Northern Railway (GNR) also advertised trips to Southwell on some of these occasions. In May 1897, for example, this company placed a notice in the *Lincolnshire Echo* for an excursion it would be running to the 'Hunt Races' at Southwell. The train started at Donington-on-Bain, Lincolnshire, picking up passengers along the way at a number of stations including Wragby and Washingborough. Eventually the Southwell Races took on such a considerable importance in the racing calendar that in 1898 it moved out to a larger venue near Rolleston. This meant it was only excursions from Mansfield which would continue to use the Southwell line and then after the Midland, the LMS and British Railways took the opportunity to run these specials.

Another popular event on the Southwell calendar for many years had been the annual agricultural show which started in 1855. On the occasion of the 25th anniversary (among others) in 1880 the Midland put on special excursions for this.

An example of how the Midland acted, in an attempt to broaden the appeal of excursions for those with different tastes, is a notice it placed in the *Derbyshire Advertiser* with the information of an excursion to Southwell on Tuesday 30th June, 1896 for a 'Grand Choral Concert'.

A view taken in the early years of the 20th century showing an eastbound passenger train at Farnsfield in the charge of a Johnson 2-4-0. *Lens of Sutton Collection*

An early postcard view of Southwell station, view looking towards Mansfield. *W. Taylor*

Chapter Three

New prospects for the line, 1890-1929

By 1899 the timetable was in some ways simplified. There were just four trains each way, weekdays only. Gone are the complications of Thursdays only/Thursdays excepted and market days. It might appear that the demand on the line from passengers was changing.

April 1899		am	am	pm	pm
Mansfield	dep.	9.45	11.00	3.20	6.15
Blidworth & Rainworth		9.55	11.10	3.31	6.24
Farnsfield		10.02	11.17	3.39	6.31
Kirklington & Edingley		10.07	11.23	3.46	6.36
Southwell		10.11	11.29	3.53	6.42
Rolleston		10.18	11.35	3.59	6.48
Newark	arr.	10.28	11.56	4.08	6.59

		am	am	pm	pm
Newark	dep.	8.20	11.32	5.10	–
Rolleston		8.29	11.54	5.26	6.58
Southwell		8.34	12.00	5.34	7.04
Kirklington & Edingley		8.42	12.07	5.42	7.11
Farnsfield		8.48	12.13	5.48	7.17
Blidworth & Rainworth		8.55	12.21	5.56	7.24
Mansfield	arr.	9.07	12.35	6.10	7.35

Four years later the timetable shows a considerable improvement in services for passengers. This may have been seen in many ways encouragingly so. However, there were some changes. The timetable issued in 1903 follows.

It would appear that in some sense the line was, in effect, now seen as two portions; the original section between Southwell and Rolleston and the section built later between Southwell and Mansfield. This would be even more apparent later.

		am	ThO* am	WO pm	ThO* pm	pm
Mansfield	dep.	9.43	10.55		3.35	6.03
Blidworth & Rainworth		9.51	11.05		3.43	6.11
Farnsfield		9.58	11.12	3.22	3.50	6.18
Kirklington & Edingley		10.03	11.18	3.28	3.55	6.23
Southwell		10.10	11.30	3.35	4.03	6.31
Rolleston	arr.	10.15	11.35	3.40	4.08	6.37
	dep.	10.18	11.45	3.50	4.10	6.42
Newark		10.26	12.00	3.58	4.17	7.50

* On other days these services operated from Southwell only in these times
ThO – Thursdays only, WO – Wednesdays only

THE MANSFIELD-SOUTHWELL-ROLLESTON RAILWAY

On the section of the line from Southwell towards Rolleston there were many additional trains.

		am	am	pm	pm	pm	pm	pm	pm	pm	pm	SO pm
Southwell	dep.	7.30	8.38	1.43	2.25	5.10	6.00	7.25	8.00	8.35	9.30	11.35
Rolleston	arr.	7.36	8.44	1.49	2.31	5.16	6.06	7.31	8.06	8.41	9.36	11.41
	dep.	7.37	9.03		2.37	5.24			8.09		9.42	11.48
Newark	arr.	7.45	9.10		2.45	5.32			8.15		9.50	11.55

SO – Saturdays only

The timetable from Newark in 1903 showed three services through to Mansfield and one which terminated at Farnsfield. There is also one service from Rolleston to Mansfield.

			ThO*	WO			ThO
		am	am	pm	pm	pm	
Newark	dep.	8.15	11.30	2.30	5.12		
Rolleston	arr.	8.23	11.38	2.37	5.18		
	dep.	8.24	11.55	2.40	5.26	6.46	
Southwell		8.30	12.00	2.46	5.31	6.52	
Kirklington & Edingley		8.36	12.07	2.53	5.38	6.59	
Farnsfield		8.42	12.13	2.59	5.44	7.05	
Blidworth & Rainworth		8.50	12.19		5.53	7.12	
Mansfield	arr.	9.00	12.31		6.02	7.24	

WO – Wednesdays only, ThO – Thursdays only.
* On other days this service ran from Newark to Southwell only, in these timings.

Additional services from Newark to Southwell,

		am	am	am	pm	pm	pm	pm	pm	pm
Newark	dep.	7.31	8.41	10.12	1.43	4.06	6.00	7.30	8.37	9.30
Rolleston	arr.	7.38	8.48	10.20	1.53	4.16	6.11	7.38	8.46	9.38
	dep.	8.02	9.06	10.27	1.59	4.20	6.18	7.44	8.50	9.46
Southwell	arr.	8.08	9.12	10.33	2.05	4.26	6.24	7.50	8.58	9.52

There were also services from Rolleston to Southwell at 1.40, 3.54, 6.46, 7.07 and 8.10 pm and an additional service on Saturdays at 11.49 am.

On the whole at this stage passengers would appear to be well catered for with these arrangements. This would seem to augur well. In a station name change, 'Kirklington & Edingley' would become just 'Kirklington' the following year in 1904.

Developments in the East Nottinghamshire coalfield

Towards the end of the 19th century the technology for mining coal had moved on to a point where it was possible to sink deeper mines and such technology was needed if the rich coal seams which are located in the east of Nottinghamshire could be worked.

The future viability and therefore the possible continued running of the Mansfield-Southwell-Rolleston line would be very much determined by one factor; the opening up of these new collieries.

In 1905 Mansfield Colliery (often referred to as 'Crown Farm Colliery') opened just to the east of Mansfield. It was the Bolsover Colliery Co., soon to become a leader in the area, which was responsible for this project. There was only one railway company in a position to service this colliery and that was the Midland. Furthermore it was in a strong position because the line from Southwell to Mansfield was a comparatively short distance away from the colliery. Given that passenger and even freight traffic along this line had not brought particularly high revenues for the company, here was an opportunity, if the line was to remain open, which might make it financially viable and more important, be the source of considerable revenue.

The mineral line, built by Hemingway & Co. for the Midland, was 1 mile 64 chains long with associated sidings and was completed by 11th January, 1905 ready to serve the colliery. It was taken off from near the area of Mansfield called 'Berry Hill' and the junction was such that entry and exit was to and from the west; in other words towards Mansfield. Moving this coal, not least with no competition, was a great boon for the Midland although it was not long before the colliery owners began to be uneasy about this monopoly in view of the rates being charged. The lack of any competition seemed to involve a higher cost than the colliery company found comfortable.

However, at least for the moment, this new traffic may well have been a saving grace for this stretch of line. For over 10 years the Midland enjoyed this monopoly before some of the owners of the developing collieries, after trying in vain to get other railway companies to service their collieries, decided to plan a railway of their own to service them. This would provide a competitive scenario.

In this period there were a number of significant developments which occurred which would impact on the Midland in this area. One was the opening of the railway just referred to, namely the Mansfield Railway from Kirkby-in-Ashfield to Clipstone via Mansfield. This line had been promoted by a group of private business individuals, several of whom had a vested interest in the coal industry and planned to open collieries in the east Nottinghamshire area. One of the motives for this group was quite clearly to break the monopoly of the Midland which, with no competitors, could pretty well fix the rates as it pleased. This situation did not always please the colliery owners and this was particularly so in the case of Mansfield Colliery. The Mansfield Railway was built over a period which included World War I and this resulted in the progress being protracted. However, by 1916 the line was up and running and as new collieries opened there was now, in some cases, the opportunity for both the Midland and the Mansfield company to serve them.

This Johnson 4-4-0 is seen having been delivered brand new to Mansfield shed. On its arrival it caused a great deal of excitement amongst the staff there. It is believed this view was recorded somewhere on the Southwell line, perhaps for crew training. *Author's Collection*

Railway staff are out in numbers when a photographer recorded the opening of Mansfield Colliery Sidings signal box and branch in 1907. *Author's Collection*

NEW PROSPECTS FOR THE LINE, 1890-1929

In order to deal with the growing amount of traffic on the line a large signal box was opened at Mansfield Colliery Junction. It would appear there were no major accidents on the line but another, which was again more of an 'incident', did attract some attention. This occurred on Tuesday 25th June, 1907 and happened at Southwell. The train for Rolleston was leaving the shed and it seems the points were changed too quickly. The outcome was that a carriage was derailed and it subsequently telescoped into the compartment directly behind it. Fortunately nobody was injured and the line was soon cleared.

The line continued to move sand for the Mansfield Sand Co. and an advertisement in the *Belper News* in 1908 lists 'the cost on rails; to Derby 2s. 10d. per ton net, Ilkeston 2s. 6d., Belper 2s. 7d.'

The second significant colliery to open in this area was Rufford Colliery in 1912. Again it was the Bolsover Colliery Co. which was the promoter. Further, again it was the Midland which was in a strong position to service this colliery and, no doubt to the satisfaction of the company, more traffic for the Mansfield to Southwell line. Suddenly the latter was proving to be a worthwhile venture after all and it was anticipated that before long there would be more to come.

A colliery at Clipstone became yet another undertaking by the Bolsover Colliery Co. It clearly seized the opportunity to expand its influence in the rich potential of the area. The company had made the decision that a start would be made as soon as coal was reached at Rufford.

This achieved, on 4th January, 1913 it was reported that the development at the Clipstone Colliery site had commenced. It was thought that about 2½ years would be needed before maximum output could be achieved but the outbreak of war the following year meant this could not be met, mainly as the result of diminished manpower as men were recruited into the armed forces. It was 1922 before Clipstone reached its full potential and by this time there had been a significant development.

As mentioned previously, in 1916 the Mansfield Railway had opened in its entirety having struggled somewhat to achieve this as a result of the war and, not least, a subsequent lack of manpower. Further it had built a branch to Rufford in 1918 which was right into the Midland's territory and there would be more incursions to follow.

An aspect which would have an impact on the railway operations in the east Nottinghamshire coalfield was the decision by the Government to carry out a major reorganization of Britain's railway system. This took effect in 1923 when it decreed that there would be just four railway companies, namely the Great Western Railway (GWR), the Southern Railway (SR), the London & North Eastern Railway (LNER) and the London Midland & Scottish Railway. The Midland Railway became part of the LMS and the Mansfield Railway became part of the LNER.

So as far as the east Nottinghamshire coalfield was concerned the two companies operating within it were now the LMS and the LNER. In some respects this would change the dynamics of the movement of coal from this area by rail. With the amount of coal to be moved by this time and eventually more to follow there was less of a sense of rivalry and on occasions, as it turned out, a good deal of co-operation. Several of the new collieries would be served by both companies and there was plenty of business for both of them.

Kirklington station *circa* 1912, view looking west. *Lens of Sutton Collection*

Kirklington station *circa* 1912 with staff (possibly the station master) and passengers in their finery. *Lens of Sutton Collection*

FURTHER GROWTH IN THE COALFIELD, 1930 TO CLOSURE   41

Midland Railway 0-6-0s Nos. 3588 and 3383 are seen in this view at Mansfield Colliery *circa* 1915. Despite obviously different boilers and cabs, both of these locomotives are members of the '1873' class. More than 900 Johnson and Deeley 0-6-0s were built for the Midland Railway. *Mansfield Museum*

In April 1923 it was announced that the Newstead Colliery Co. had made the decision to sink a mine at Blidworth. The main objective was to reach a thick seam known as the Barnsley Bed which it was stated 'invariably produces a six feet thickness of steam coal on a seam varying between eight and ten foot [*sic*] in thickness.' It was pointed out that 'the new colliery would be linked up with the Mansfield and Southwell branch railway.' This was clearly more good news for the LMS with relatively easy access possible in view of its proximity to this new colliery. Even so the LNER would also seek a share in this business. However, there would prove to be problems and it would not turn out to be plain sailing for the Newstead Colliery Co.

The LMS was ready to work with the LNER when it came to servicing the Blidworth Colliery although there had been protracted negotiations. The LMS would charge the LNER with an easement of £50 to take its Rufford Colliery branch from the former Mansfield Railway over its line to Blidworth but this was not a real issue. Discussions had been held over the matter of shared facilities at the colliery itself. Eventually the outcome was an arrangement that the running road and the loop to the empty wagon sidings and the necessary signal box and signalling would be constructed and maintained at joint equal cost with the LNER. There would also be equal rights of ownership on this section. It was agreed that the LNER branch would commence with a junction from the Rufford Colliery branch and terminate by a junction with the joint running road to the

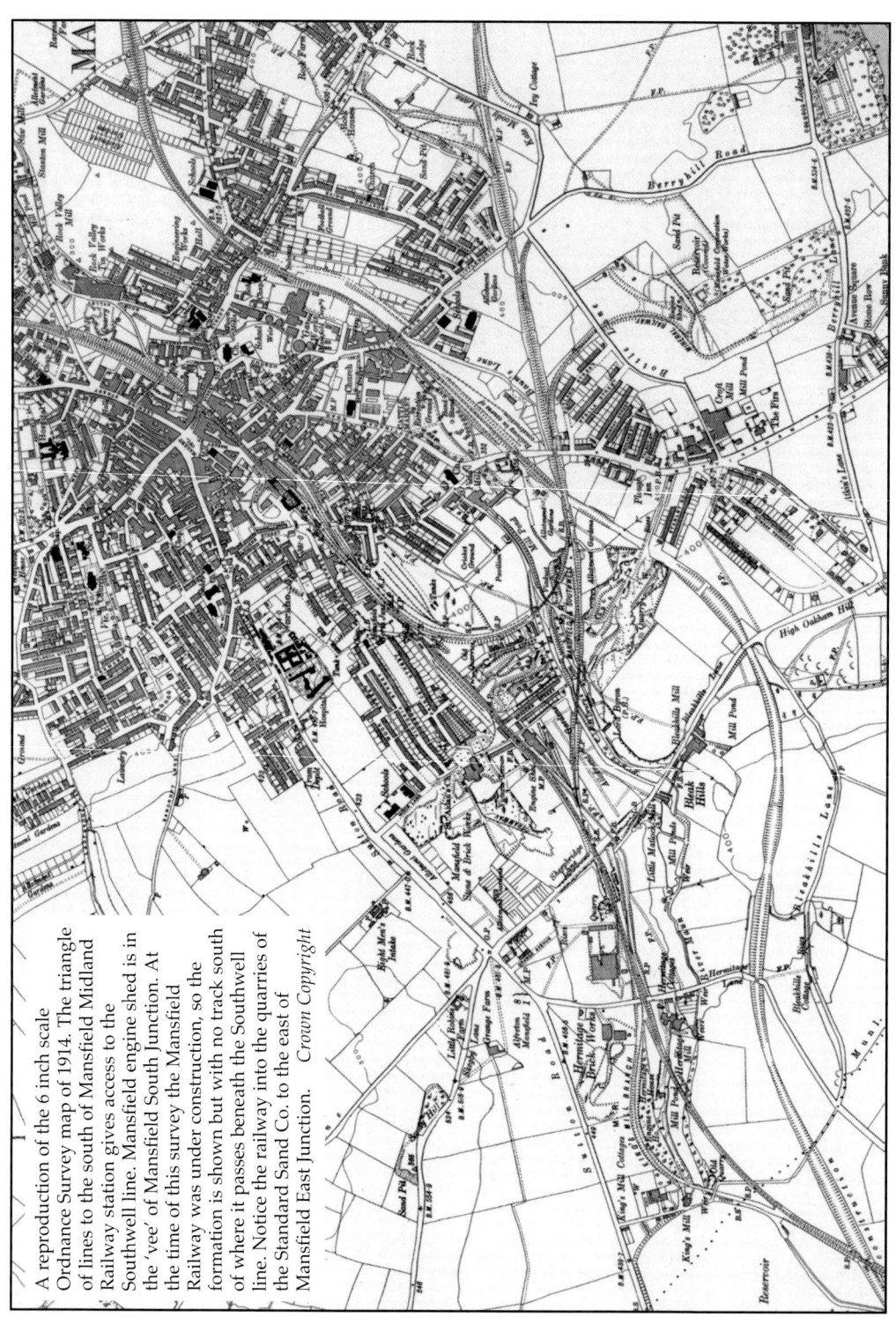

A reproduction of the 6 inch scale Ordnance Survey map of 1914. The triangle of lines to the south of Mansfield Midland Railway station gives access to the Southwell line. Mansfield engine shed is in the 'vee' of Mansfield South Junction. At the time of this survey the Mansfield Railway was under construction, so the formation is shown but with no track south of where it passes beneath the Southwell line. Notice the railway into the quarries of the Standard Sand Co. to the east of Mansfield East Junction. *Crown Copyright*

NEW PROSPECTS FOR THE LINE, 1890-1929

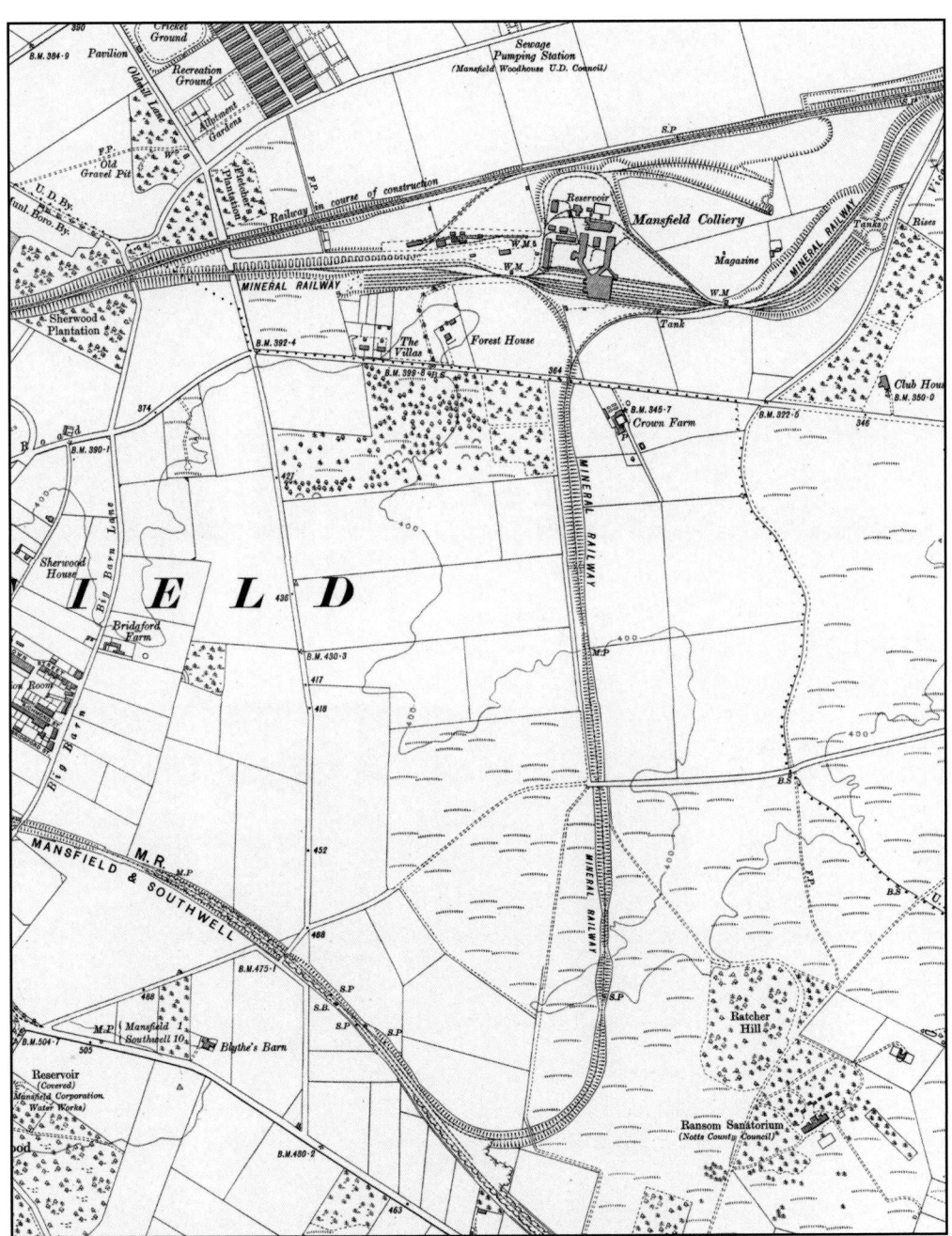

A reproduction of the 6 inch scale Ordnance Survey map of 1913 of the Mansfield Colliery branch. The Mansfield Railway is seen at the top, 'in the course of construction'. *Crown Copyright*

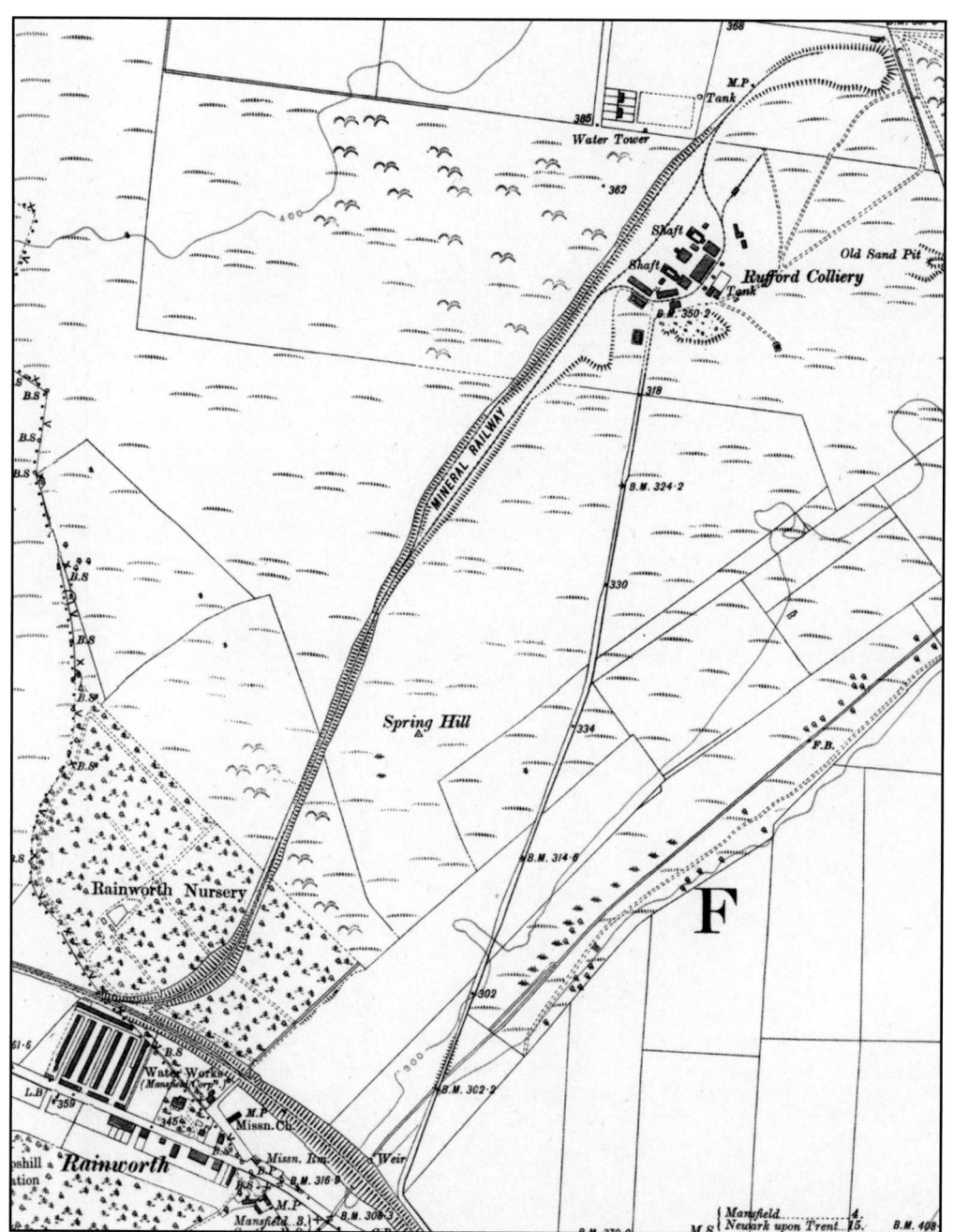

A reproduction of the 6 inch scale Ordnance Survey map of 1913 of the Rufford Colliery branch.
Crown Copyright

NEW PROSPECTS FOR THE LINE, 1890-1929

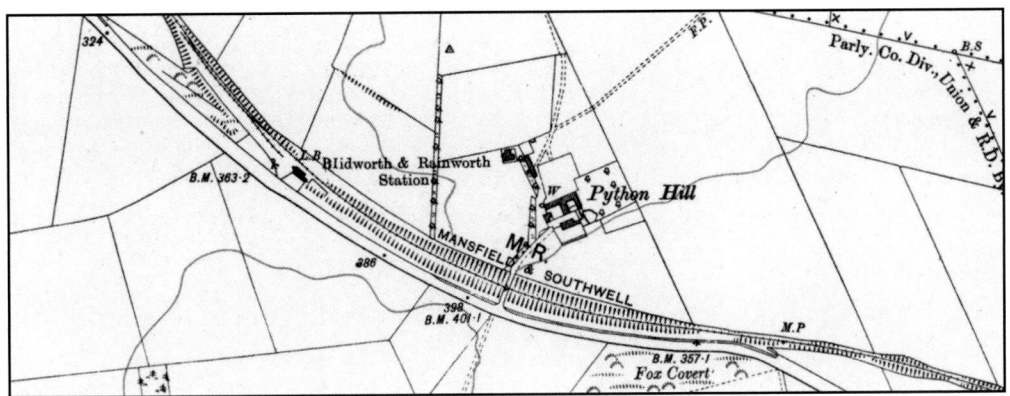
A reproduction of the 6 inch scale Ordnance Survey map of 1913 of Blidworth station.
Crown Copyright

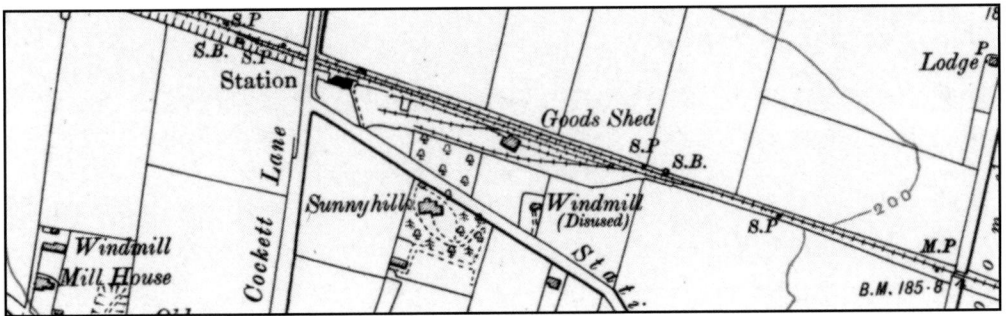
A reproduction of the 6 inch scale Ordnance Survey map of 1915 of Farnsfield station.
Crown Copyright

A reproduction of the 6 inch scale Ordnance Survey map of 1915 of Kirklington station.
Crown Copyright

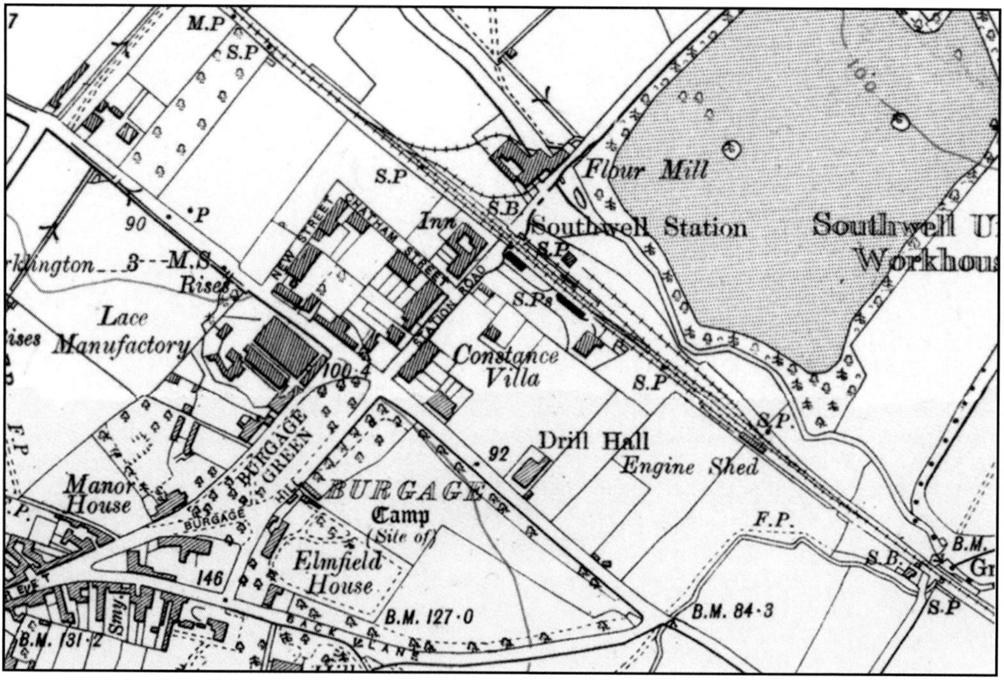

A reproduction of the 6 inch scale Ordnance Survey map of 1915 of Southwell station and its environs.
Crown Copyright

A reproduction of the 6 inch scale Ordnance Survey map of 1915 of Rolleston Junction station with the line from Mansfield and Southwell coming in from the west meeting the Nottingham and Lincoln route. Note the racecourse (*top left*).
Crown Copyright

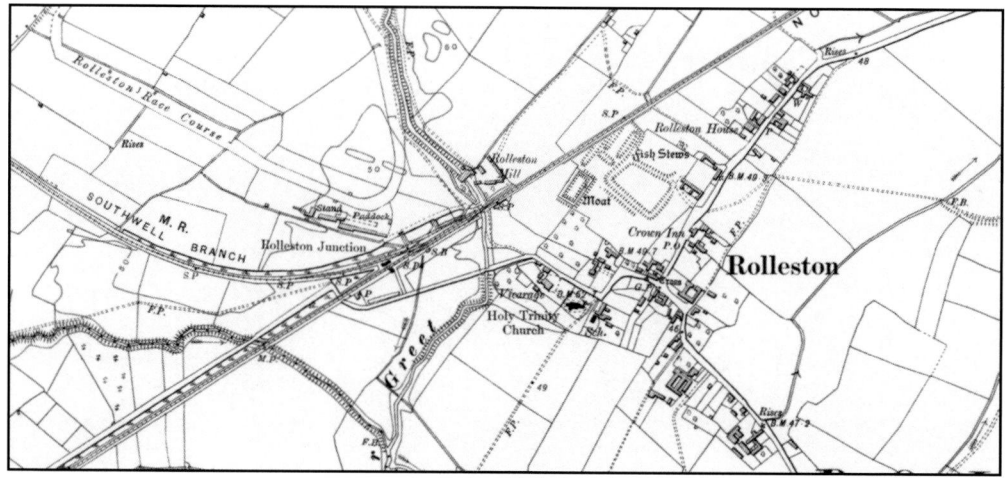

sidings, just described. The Newstead Colliery Co., which was responsible for the actual sinking and operating of the colliery, would pay for further siding accommodation for loaded and empty wagons. It was reckoned that 3,000 tons of coal would be moved daily once it was opened. Certain unforeseeable circumstances would result in that not being for some time.

Once again, even though by this time the name of the station at Rainworth had been changed from Blidworth to Blidworth & Rainworth, certainly for timetabling purposes, the station sited at Rainworth was still being referred to in LMS circles as Blidworth. In September 1924 the LMS placed a contract with Messrs Logan & Hemingway for the construction of a single line of railway at the loop at Blidworth to be completed by July 1925,

> For a further branch from the Mansfield to Southwell line with the starting point about half a mile east of Blidworth station. The line will run to the new Blidworth Colliery a distance of about a mile from the other line and there would be extensive excavation of sandstone with a bridge over the main road from Mansfield to Southwell. It is anticipated that fifty men will take about eleven months.

Further on 16th December, 1925 the LMS announced a series of new contracts. These included 'the reconstruction of Blidworth station'. As far as the movement of sand was concerned, the Mansfield Sand Co. announced that its sand could now be taken by rail to any station.

By now there had been rapid progress with the sinking of Blidworth Colliery and on 13th January, 1926, a top hard seam 3 ft 7 in. had been reached in No. 2 shaft at a depth of 721 yards. The Union Jack was flown to mark this significant event and there was something of a sense of relief. The reason for this was that it had not been deemed necessary to make any trial holes before the 'sinkers', used to make the shaft, had been put to work. The boring had gone considerably deeper than that needed at neighbouring mines and there were those who started to doubt whether coal would be reached. However, reached it eventually was, in No. 2 shaft. No. 1 shaft, which had reached 677 yards, had to be taken deeper. By this time the LMS had practically completed its branch to the colliery and although work on the LNER scheme had just started it was proceeding well. The LMS had not met with any problems but another problem of a different nature arose.

In the meantime, in February 1926 there was a move to extend the coalfield in the area. A private Bill was deposited at the House of Commons and the petitioners included the Duke of Portland, Southwell Rural District Council and the Butterley Company.

The LMS also introduced a Bill which contained proposals regarding extra servicing of 'local collieries' and these included Rufford Colliery. There was opposition to this, the main opponents being the Butterley Company and the LNER.

This pressed ahead and on 2nd March, 1926 there was a special meeting at Euston of the LMS shareholders. The purpose of the meeting was to seek approval 'for certain Bills and orders in accordance with the Standing Orders of Parliament and with the rules under the Light Railways Act'. One of these would be,

An official photograph taken in 1928 showing the construction of the new bridge carrying the LNER Blidworth Colliery line over the LMS's Southwell line. *LNER*

> … a Bill to empower the Company to acquire from the present owners a short length of railway known as the Rufford Colliery Railway serving Rufford Colliery and it was intended to use it for the purpose of carrying the traffic of another colliery 'known as the Clipstone Colliery.

Clearly it was the aim of the LMS to have a share of the rewards to be had in the transportation of coal from these new collieries. These would, without doubt add to the viability of the Mansfield to Southwell railway line; indeed there was something of a reversal of priorities here as the line became the key element if the coalfield was to be serviced to the benefit of the LMS. The Act for this was placed on the statute book on 30th June, 1926 (16 & 17 Geo. 5 ch. xxxii). There was also a motion to support a Bill for a project called 'The Mid-Nottinghamshire Joint Railway' and this it was reported would be promoted jointly 'by this company and the London and N.E. Railway [sic].'

The Mid-Nottinghamshire Joint Railway

It was reported in April that the proposal to build the Mid-Nottinghamshire Joint Railway had been under discussion in the House of Lords and the necessary legislation which had at one point been keenly disputed, had been passed. The Act (16 and 17 Geo. 5 ch. xlv) is dated 15th July, 1926. The 'keen dispute' resulted in the Act being a very lengthy document which runs into 66 pages and the choice is made to describe 'The London Midland and Scottish Railway' simply as 'The Midland' and 'The London and North Eastern Railway' simply as 'The North Eastern Railway'. The Act authorizes a joint venture by the LMS and LNER companies. The project would be overseen by a joint committee of Directors appointed by these two companies. Much of the thinking behind the scheme was an intention to serve collieries which it was envisaged would open in the vicinity of Calverton and also Bothamsall. The original plan was to build a line to run from Bestwood Park Junction, south of Hucknall, via Farnsfield and on to Ollerton and thereafter to join the line between Worksop and Retford at the northern end. However, it transpired that only part of the line was built. This was the section between Farnsfield and Ollerton. A colliery was not built at Bothamsall, although much later one was sunk at Bevercotes and the 'northern' section of the line was modified somewhat to serve it. (For many years until this happened there was a large embankment which stopped short at the road linking New Ollerton to Walesby, seemingly waiting for a bridge to be built over the road.) In the initial scheme it was reported 922,000 cubic yards of earth would have to be moved and 24 bridges and a viaduct would be needed. There would be 18 miles of fencing to be put in place.

Competition for passenger traffic

Whilst all this activity was taking place, it would seem that the level of passenger traffic on the line between Southwell and Mansfield was dwindling.

Back in 1924 it was reported that 240 'omnibuses' were licensed for use in Mansfield and district and only a year later so rapid was the growth that the number had increased to 408, although of these, 10 were charabancs and 60 were taxis. The companies with the majority of the omnibuses were Trent Motor Traction and Underwoods (later to become the East Midland Motor Services). In addition, by this time, bus companies were required to provide proper timetables to meet the conditions for licensing and so a properly structured service was emerging. This was proving a real threat to rail services.

Slowly but surely bus companies such as Mansfield & District Tramways were making even further advances in services and with the added flexibility of where these vehicles could stop and pick up passengers, there was a greater appeal for the travelling public. In April the bus company placed an announcement in the local press to the effect that there would be an additional service on Sundays between Mansfield and Newark, signs of growth.

Bridges over Nottingham Road, Mansfield. The nearer of the bridges is the Mansfield Railway (Great Central) line, with the Southwell branch bridge in the distance. Notice the tram track and wires of the Mansfield & District Tramways route to Berryhill. The trams were replaced by buses in 1932. *W. Taylor Collection*

Almost in contrast, the timetable for passenger services being issued for the Mansfield-Southwell-Rolleston line, as far as those for the local press was concerned, had become basic, to say the least.

Whilst timetables for other lines had the usual format, on 11th June, 1927, this is all that prospective travellers on the Mansfield to Southwell Railway were given:

Trains leave Mansfield at 9.20 am and 4.15 pm, Southwell at 9.54 am and 4.50 pm Newark [arr.] at 10.10 am and 5.05 pm.
Trains leave Newark at 7.50 am and 5.25 pm, Southwell at 8.12 am and 5.38 pm Mansfield [arr.] at 8.50 am and 6.13 pm.

This basic timetable gave no details about a Southwell to Rolleston service. Not particularly helpful for those travelling to the intermediate stations. The reduction in services since the timetable issued 20 years previously was, no doubt, reflecting this marked change in the travelling habits of the general public and the company probably already thinking that a significant change was in the air. The number of people travelling on these trains is not made clear but speculation might lead to the conclusion that it was not large.

Further developments in the coalfield

At the Stanton Ironworks Company's colliery at Bilsthorpe, coal was reached by August. This colliery was able to claim having the most up-to-date facilities in the country. There were two shafts, each 20 ft in diameter and 500 yds deep, with these shafts being lined with concrete down to a depth of 300 yds, necessary because the ground was so wet. Electricity was generated on site by mixed pressure steam turbines each generating 1,500 kilowatts. Although coal was being mined by the beginning of September, some work was incomplete. The screening and washing plants were only partly operational and the pit-head baths had not been finished.

In November, the Parliamentary agents to the LMS deposited a General Powers Bill to be introduced into Parliament by that company in the next session. The Bill comprised 34 clauses under which power was sought to construct about 1½ miles of new railway in Nottinghamshire. This was to make a curve at Farnsfield to connect the Mansfield to Southwell railway with the Mid-Nottinghamshire Joint Railway.

The LMS was after, not least, a share of the output of coal at Bilsthorpe which the former Mansfield Railway, now part of the LNER, was already enjoying. The objective was not a particularly aggressive or competitive one, simply one of having a share of the business of moving this coal.

It was observed that 'this short length of line is noteworthy as being the only new line for which powers will be sought next session by any of the grouped railways and that no new powers are sought by this Bill'. The anticipated cost was £53,850.

When the Bill eventually came up for consideration there were some matters which had to be resolved and there was an objection. Some properties were affected by the building of this curve. One mentioned was Cockett's Farm where a severance would necessitate accommodation work to enable passage from one side of the railway to the other. This was not seen to be difficult and therefore not a problem.

However, there was an objection raised to the project. It was pointed out that there was a possibility of reducing 'sporting amenities' of the Hexgreave Estate by between 100 and 200 acres and it was argued that if the scheme went ahead compensation would be necessary and this would need to be assessed. It was also said that the matter of colliery access was questionable because there was still no real evidence of the Babbington Colliery Co. and the Wigan Coal & Iron Co. pressing ahead with sinking collieries at Oxton and Bothamsall. Also, that the LNER already serviced Bilsthorpe, Ollerton and Thoresby collieries. However, it was argued for the Bill to be passed that the LMS wished to gain access to these collieries and to do it in 'a most suitable way'. It was argued that if the powers sought were granted the curve would be built in conjunction with the LNER which may well choose to make use of it. It had the advantage of giving access to favourable gradients and low traffic density between Farnsfield and Beeston via Rolleston 'compared with other routes'. Mr Charteris QC for the Hexgreave Estates argued that if the curve was constructed it would 'sterilise' the property of his clients and 'would do away with the coal on the property'. He saw the development 'causing hardship, unnecessary harassment and inconsiderate interference with the interests and rights' of the estate. Even so, after consideration of these various factors and in spite of them, the Bill was passed and construction of the curve was allowed to go ahead.

Back at Blidworth, the colliery was now nearing completion. However, in August 1928 the Newstead Colliery Co. suddenly announced that the mine would close 'for an indefinite period'. The reason given in a statement issued on 22nd August, was that the depression in trade would make it inappropriate to remain open and the contractors were requested to terminate their work. This obviously came as a blow. Both the LMS and the LNER had to face the problem about what action should be taken given this situation. Some work did continue.

At an LMS Board meeting in January 1929 it is was reported that more passenger and freight miles had been run 'since the end of the war'. That seemed to be the good news. However, it was also pointed out that the increase in passenger miles had come about mainly through running more excursion trains and to some extent - and here was the caveat - this new traffic had been able to make up for 'the loss to the roads'. Furthermore it was short distance traffic (on the railway) that had seen the biggest impact from 'road competition'. It was pointed out that nevertheless this traffic still represented a large element of the company's receipts and so far regular services had not been reduced.

A comment was made that 'people in the country were definitely poorer and will have less to spend on railway travel'. It might have felt that things were just holding up but eventually there was worse to come.

The company announced that it intended to spend £200,000 on improving its activities associated with the way it would transport coal in the Nottinghamshire coalfield. In fact the scheme, it pointed out, was well underway. 'There would be more modern and expeditious transport for Nottinghamshire collieries' and it stated that these would help the coal industry in the area. It was also pointed out that a new loop at Kirklington had already been completed and other schemes would include the doubling of the railway between Upton crossing and Rolleston West Junction together with a new west curve at Rolleston connecting the Mansfield and Southwell line with the Lincoln to Nottingham route. There would also be additional siding accommodation provided at Mansfield Colliery and Rufford Colliery. The loop at Farnsfield would be extended. It was pointed out that the purpose of much of this work was to enable London and other southbound traffic from some of these mid-Nottinghamshire collieries to be worked through the new curve at Rolleston with the advantage that heavier trains could be used on this route rather than through Kirkby because the gradients were more favourable. The west junction at Rolleston onto the Nottingham-Newark line which would enable this was opened during April. Clearly the emphasis as far as the Mansfield-Southwell line was concerned, was now on the movement of coal and with access to only two of the new collieries in the developing area of the Nottinghamshire coalfield the company was determined to capitalize on it.

The axe falls on Mansfield-Southwell passenger services

As noted earlier, with the internal combustion engine on the ascendancy and bus services very much on the increase decisions would have to be made. So although there might have been a note of hope in the comments made at the LMS meeting in January, clearly things had not improved. With this competition of road traffic continuing to grow and with the impact reckoned to be getting more severe and certainly there being no likelihood of this trend changing, the LMS decided the time had come to act. On 12th August, 1929 it announced 'the closure of the branch from Mansfield to Southwell to passenger traffic'.

To off-set this a statement was issued that there would be 'a new omnibus service in conjunction with Trent Motor Traction Co. which is one of the road transport undertakings included in the provisional agreement between the LMS and LNE companies.' There appears to have been little public reaction to this closure.

The section between Southwell and Rolleston, however, would still retain its passenger facility. This service consisted of a Johnson '1P' class 0-4-4T introduced by the Midland as far back as 1881. It ran with one coach on the 'push-pull' principle and came to be referred to locally as 'The Paddy'. However, it would seem that the LMS had taken something of an aversion to the term 'push-pull' when referring to this system and decided a more fitting description would be 'motor train'. As will be seen it would operate well beyond the Midland period and it would see out the LMS as well. There was a weekly change of stock for this one-coach train which would see many days of useful service.

On the one hand, the Midland with its reticence to build the line because it was probably convinced it would not be cost-effective, had, it might be argued, been ultimately justified even though it could not have fully anticipated the development of the motor vehicle which rendered it so. However, there had been a major change in circumstances and could well have meant that it might have resulted in the complete closure of the line. The situation had been changing with a development which would prove this was certainly not going to be the case.

... but race specials continue

Long after passenger services had ceased, the race specials could be seen making their way along the line and as late as 1937 they were still stopping at the intermediate stations which were normally closed when general passenger traffic was withdrawn.

An advertisement in the press in this period reads:

SOUTHWELL RACES
September 18th

Mansfield depart 1.15   Blidworth 1.30   Farnsfield 1.38
Return 6.30 pm

The sight of a 'passenger train' running on the Southwell line well into the 1950s held a certain excitement for young (and perhaps not so young) rail enthusiasts!

A busy scene at Southwell racecourse *circa* 1920. The Nottingham-Lincoln line can be seen in the background. Rolleston Junction station building is to the right.   *Nottingham Post*

Along the line

With the line between Mansfield and Southwell closed to passenger traffic in 1929, the only persons thereafter who would experience 'a trip down the line' would be the train crews and other railway employees apart from those who travelled on the 'Race Specials' or the occasional excursion.

Many years later, as will be seen, the possibility to experience some of this journey in a very different way would become possible.

From the Midland station at Mansfield the train would leave on the up line and almost immediately turn off on the North Junction and following this, the East Junction. It would then cross the A60 road linking Mansfield to Nottingham. It would head in a generally easterly direction on the single track, skirting Mansfield and after one mile would pass the first sand quarry which had sidings linked to the railway. Mansfield sand was still very much in demand in foundries. Shortly afterwards it crossed the main road linking Mansfield with Newark (A617). Just beyond this on its south side it skirted the Forest Hospital, opened in 1893 and often referred to locally as the 'Fever Hospital' where for many years in its two departments, patients with diphtheria and scarlet fever were isolated and treated. The line now turned in a more south - easterly direction and entered a further cutting emerging at a point just before where a branch went off to Mansfield Colliery. The distance travelled now being two miles. At this point there was also a small sand quarry (labelled as 'Sills') with a short siding to serve it. Away to the left was Ling Forest a large area of open scrub land which at certain times of year was covered in purple blossom.

Beyond this could be seen a raised area called Strawberry Hill (known locally as 'Strawberry Knob'). The line now followed the general direction of the A617. Just before reaching Rainworth there was a branch line to Rufford Colliery. In Rainworth, at the time, the main road split, with the A617 going on to meet the A614. After passing over the A617, the railway ran alongside the minor road. The first station on the line was at Rainworth with the distance travelled now being about four miles. As mentioned previously this station was first designated Rainworth, then Blidworth although Blidworth was well over a mile away and latterly it became Blidworth and Rainworth. The platform was on the south side and there was a small goods yard. Ignoring a strict chronological sequence, just beyond the station there was a branch to the south to Blidworth Colliery.

The line then passed into open countryside, typified by the rural nature of this area with agriculture forming an important aspect of the region. After having passed over the main road linking Doncaster with Leicester (A614) and further on through this farmland with its farm houses, the train, having travelled a further 3½ miles, would arrive at Farnsfield, the second station on the line. This station, with platforms on both sides of the line and which at this point included a passing loop, was on the north side of the village and had a small marshalling yard with a goods warehouse. The line continued in an easterly direction and after passing a short siding on the north side for Newark Corporation Water Works, reached 'Kirklington and Edingley', the last station

NEW PROSPECTS FOR THE LINE, 1890-1929

before Southwell, this section of the journey being approximately two miles. The station Kirklington & Edingley was at neither; Kirklington being about a mile to the north of it and Edingley being about the same distance to the south of the line. It eventually became 'Kirklington'. There was one platform on the north side of the line with no siding facility.

Moving on through similar terrain in a south-easterly direction and after about two miles, the train arrived at Southwell station which was situated to the east of the town. There was a short siding here for Caudwell's Mill.

As mentioned previously, Southwell might be seen as the railway centre for the line, having coaling, water and siding facilities and also an engine shed. There were platforms on either side of a short double section of line (to Rolleston Junction). Leaving Southwell and once over the level crossing the line reached Rolleston where there was the last station. Here there was a junction with the line from Nottingham to Newark and Lincoln. Both lines had two platforms giving Rolleston a total of four.

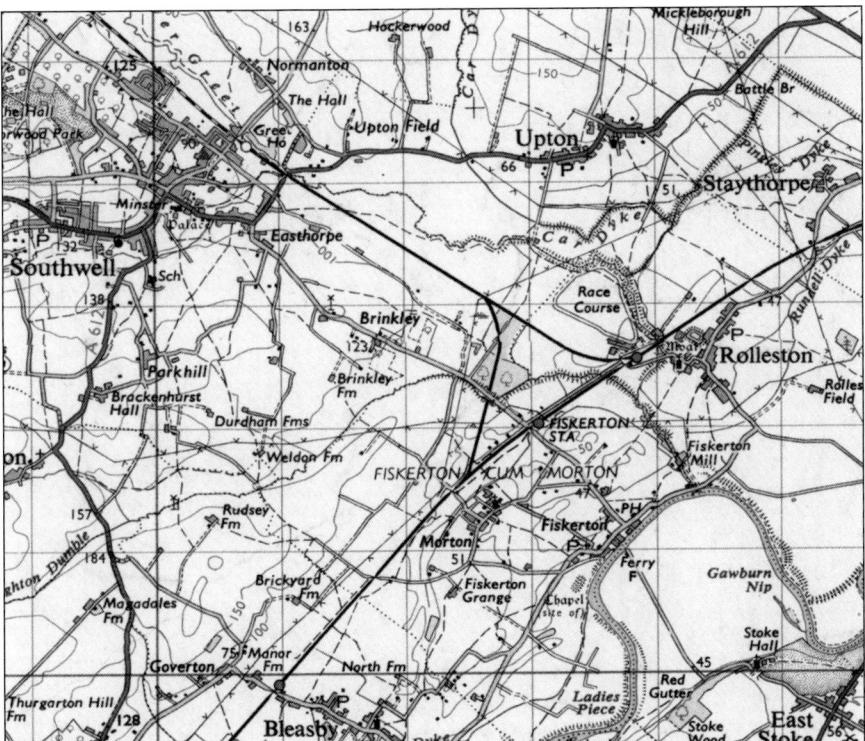

The 1960 Ordnance Survey map shows Rolleston south curve, added in 1929, forming a route from Blidworth and Bilsthorpe collieries to Nottingham, which avoided routing trains via Kirkby-in-Ashfield. The new curve eased traffic flow and offered a route with easier gradients for loaded trains. The curve was taken out of use on 1st March, 1965.

Crown Copyright

An unidentified ex-MR class '3F' 0-6-0 heads a coal train from one of the Mansfield area collieries as it approaches Rolleston West Junction whose bracket signal arm shows the points set towards the main Lincoln-Nottingham line which it will shortly join facing south-west.

Roland Hoggard

Taken from the steps of the Rolleston West Junction signal box, as was the previous image, the photographer has turned around to capture the same train, composed entirely of wooden-bodied wagons, some being private owner wagons, as it complied with the regulation 15 mph speed limit in this 1930s view. The middle of the train is crossing the line to Rolleston Junction station.

Roland Hoggard

Having photographed the coal train Roland Hoggard has taken the opportunity to photograph Rolleston West Junction signal box including his father, who was a signalman there, also in view.   *Roland Hoggard*

The 30-lever signal box at Fiskerton Junction was built in Midland Railway-style and opened with the Rolleston south curve on 7th April, 1929. The building beyond the gates contained an 8-lever ground frame. Known as Morton Crossing, the ground frame gave the option to switch the signal box out during quiet periods. Seen here on 12th January, 1993, the signal box and manually-operated crossing gates survived until 2015.   *Mick King*

Chapter Four

Further growth in the coalfield, 1930 to closure

It was in September 1932 that the company owning Blidworth Colliery intimated that it would re-open the mine although it was anticipated output, certainly initially, would be small. At this stage the colliery company continued to question the wisdom of completing the branch. However, as production rose, an output of 250,000 tons per annum was achieved. The LMS was in a comparatively strong position and the LNER reckoned that as there was very little work to be done to finish its line and a considerable quantity of this coal could be destined for places on its system and beyond, the time was right and completion was effected. This was done in the first half of 1934. On another front it was reported in 1935 that the quantity of sand being moved by the railway had completely displaced imported sands.

By 1937 the Southwell line was seeing brisk business with coal traffic and the operation had to be closely monitored in terms of traffic movements particularly around the collieries. The following are the directions issued in this period by the LMS for these movements and associated practices.

Mansfield Colliery Junction
No vehicles must be allowed to stand upon the main line at this place without an engine being attached and the rear portion of trains from Southwell having to attach or detach traffic at Mansfield Colliery Sidings must be placed in one of the sidings.

Trains from Southwell to Mansfield must not attach or detach at the new connection at the Southwell end of Mansfield Colliery Sidings.

Mansfield Colliery Branch
The single line between Mansfield Colliery Signal Box and Mansfield is worked as a siding.

Only one engine in steam or two engines coupled together, which are then to be treated as one train, must be allowed on the Mansfield Colliery side of the signal on the colliery side of the loop siding.

During the time a train is on the Colliery side of the signal on the Colliery side of the loop siding, drivers of trains entering the loop siding may *when authorised by the signalman to do so* take their engines from the loop siding on to the single line and return to Mansfield Colliery Junction signal box on that line for the purpose of running round their trains but must only proceed on to the single line as far as is necessary to take the engine clear of the loop siding points.

Drivers from Mansfield Colliery to Mansfield Colliery Junction signal box must keep a good look-out when approaching the signal on the colliery side of the loop siding and must be prepared to stop short of any obstruction that may exist on the single line between that signal and the signal box.

Should a train require assistance (or any special circumstances render it necessary to send a second engine down) the fireman must proceed to the Mansfield Colliery Junction signal box and inform the signalman who must, on receipt of such information allow a second engine to be on the line on the Colliery side of the signal on the Colliery side of the loop siding.

The second engine must be accompanied by the fireman of the disabled train, who must explain to the driver where his train is and in what circumstances it is situated.

The guard of the disabled train will be responsible for the safe and proper working of the line until both engines have left and it is again clear.

FURTHER GROWTH IN THE COALFIELD, 1930 TO CLOSURE

All vehicles must be taken in front of the engine from Mansfield Colliery Junction to the Mansfield Colliery. A brake van must be in front of the wagons and a sufficient number of wagon brakes must be applied near the brake van to enable to descend the incline and be brought to a stand before reaching the gate at the junction of the lines leading to the Colliery Loaded and Empty Wagon Sidings which must always be kept locked across the Branch except when required to be opened for a train to pass.

The points between the Mansfield Empty Wagon Sidings and the screen lines must be kept locked open for the screen lines except when required to be unlocked to allow a train to pass. Trains proceeding to these sidings must be brought to stand clear of the points to allow the guard to unlock them.

Between Mansfield and Farnsfield
An engine must be at the end of all trains stopping to attach vehicles on the intermediate sidings between the Mansfield East Junction and Mansfield Colliery Junction.

Rufford Colliery Branch
The points between the Rufford Colliery Empty Wagon Sidings and the screen lines must be kept locked open for the screen lines and trains proceeding to the Empty Wagon Sidings must be brought to a stand clear of the points to allow the guard to unlock them.

Blidworth Junction
No vehicle must be allowed to stand on the main line at Blidworth Junction unless attached to an engine.

Blidworth Colliery Branch
The L. & N.E. Company have joint running powers over the Empty Wagon Branch from the junction with their line.

Vehicles not exceeding 50 in number from the L.M.S. line for the Empty Wagon Branch may be propelled from Blidworth Junction or from the loop line opposite the Loaded Wagon Sidings but drivers of such trains must bring their engine to a stand at the first 'stop' board from the Blidworth Junction end and not proceed until the Klaxon horn has been sounded. Drivers of trains with the engine leading may proceed as far as the second stop board from the Blidworth Junction end where the train must be brought to a stand and not proceed until receipt of a hand signal from the guard or shunter.

On the train being brought to a stand the guard or shunter must obtain the Blidworth Colliery Branch staff and place it in the slot in the Blidworth Colliery ground frame in order to release the Empty Wagon Branch staff, which is locked in the ground lever frame when not in use. All trains proceeding to the Empty Wagon Sidings must be brought to a stand clear of the points connecting with the screen lines to allow the guard to unlock them.

To prevent vehicles running away from the Empty Wagon Sidings on to the branch, the points leading to the Empty Wagon Sidings to the screen lines must always be kept open for the screen lines except when required to be unlocked to allow a train to pass between the Branch and the Empty Wagon Sidings.

Engines returning from the Empty Wagon Sidings must not proceed past the 'stop' board situated beyond the run-round loop until the guard, shunter or fireman has replaced the Empty Wagon Branch staff in the ground frame and obtained the staff for the L.M.S. or L.& N.E. line as the case may be.

Clipstone Colliery Branch
The points leading from the Empty Wagon Sidings to the screen lines must be kept locked open for the screen lines, except when required to be unlocked to allow a train to pass between the Branch and the Empty Wagon Siding and trains for these sidings and must be brought to a stand clear of the connection with the screen lines to enable the guard to unlock the points and ascertain that the line is clear.

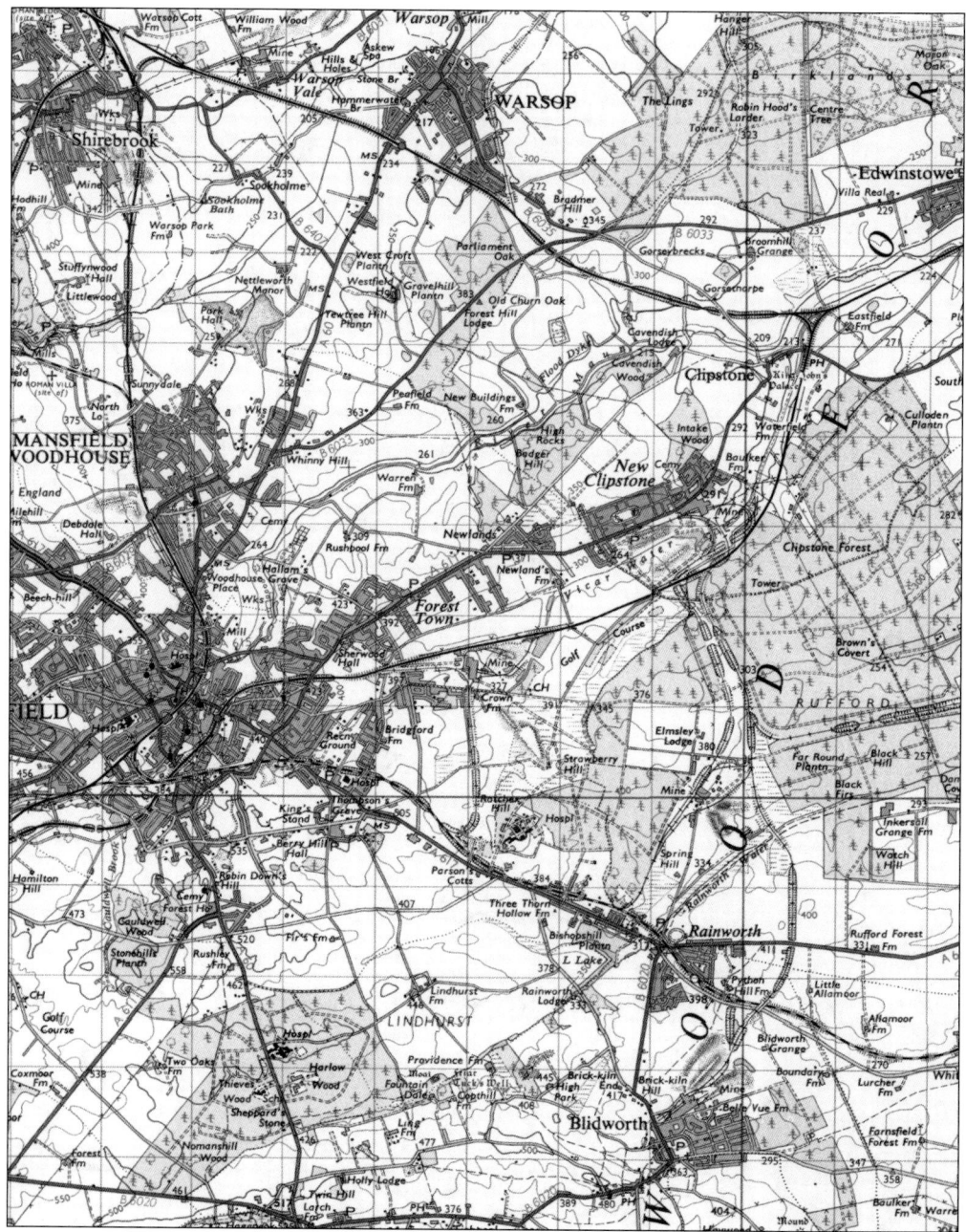

The 1960 Ordnance Survey map which shows rail connections to the various collieries from the main line railways in the area east of Mansfield including the LNER-built Blidworth Colliery line and its line to Bilsthorpe Colliery (*opposite page*). *Crown Copyright*

FURTHER GROWTH IN THE COALFIELD, 1930 TO CLOSURE

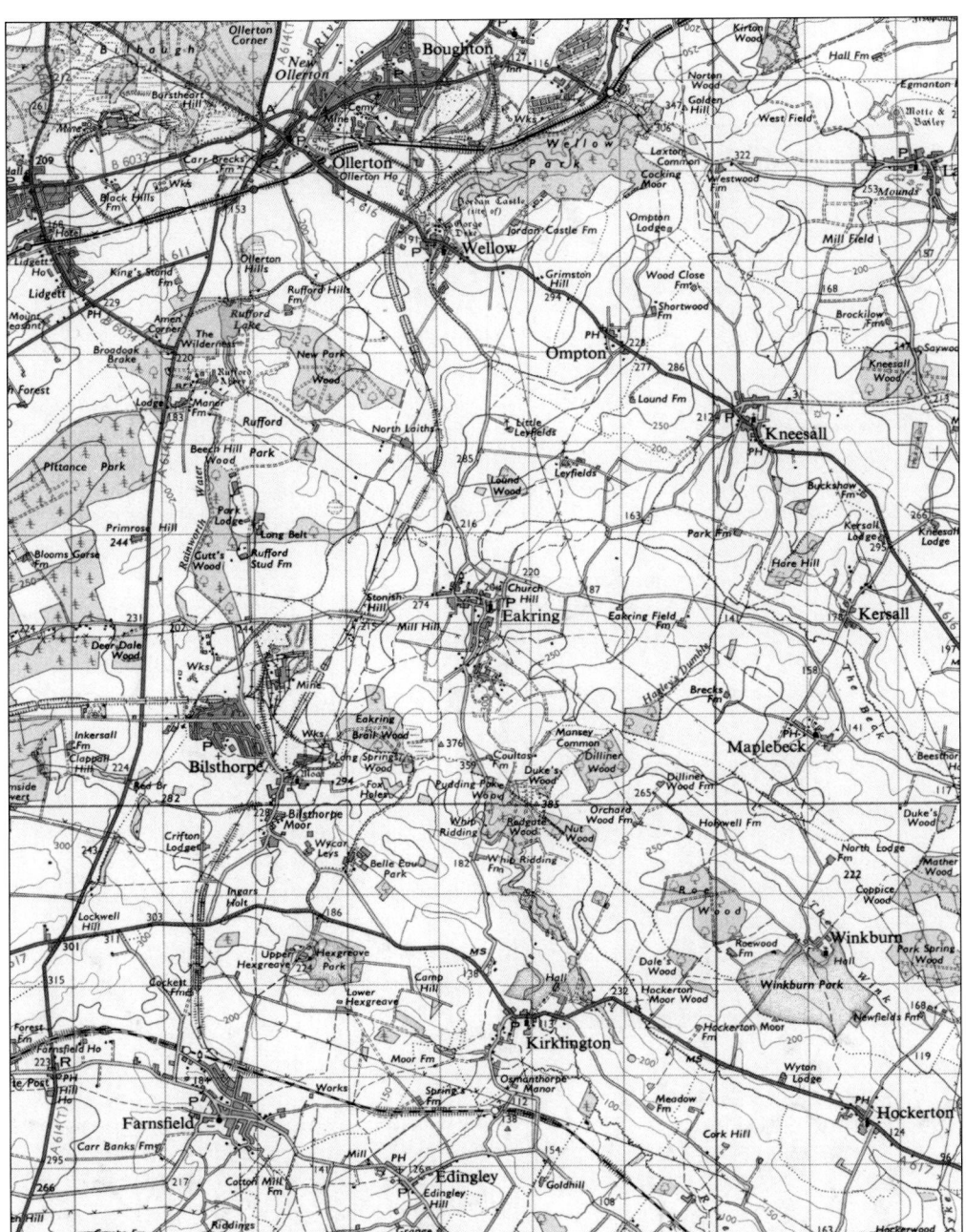

The Ordnance Survey map from 1960 showing the Mid-Nottinghamshire Joint line to Bilsthorpe and Ollerton from Farnsfield. *Crown Copyright*

The Elmsley level crossing gates must be kept locked across the railway with the chain and lock provided for the purpose and up and down trains must be brought to a stand clear of the crossing to enable the guard or shunter (the fireman in the case of a light engine) to unlock the gates and place them across the roadway. When the train has passed over the crossing it must again be brought to a stand until the gates have been placed and locked across the railway.

When a shunter travels with the train he must ride upon the engine to the gates, then proceeding forward on the engine; when the train has passed over the crossing the guard must close and lock the gates.

The key for the gates must be kept with the staff.

Between Farnsfield and Kirklington
Newark Corporation Waterworks Siding
Trains must not stop at this siding for traffic purposes unless there is an engine at the Kirklington end of the train.

Bilsthorpe Colliery Empty Wagons Branch
All wagons must be taken in front of the engine from the Bilsthorpe Colliery Empty Wagon Run-Round Loop.

The signal giving permission for trains to enter the Empty Wagon Sidings must be worked by guards and shunters from the stage at the Empty Wagons Siding.

When wagons are left either on the running line or the run-round loop the guard or shunter in charge must pin down a sufficient number of wagon brakes to prevent the wagons running away.

Wheel scotches are provided.

The outbreak of World War II saw the railway system being brought under Government control (The Power of the Regulation of Forces Act) with various priorities resulting in the changes to timetables and procedures. 'The Paddy', however, continued to run throughout the war, plying between Southwell and Rolleston Junction. The following is from the 'Emergency Passenger Services' timetable issued by the LMS in September, 1939. It remains a comparatively comprehensive service.

Southwell-Rolleston Junction with connections to Newark
One class only between Southwell and Rolleston Junction

Weekdays only		am	am	am	am	am	am
Southwell	dep.	7.20	7.45	8.15	8.53	9.24	9.51
Rolleston Junction	arr.	7.25*	7.50	8.20	8.58†	9.29	9.56
	dep.		7.58	8.21		9.34	
Newark	arr.		8.05	8.29		9.41	

* Gives convenient connections at Rolleston Junction to both Lincoln and Nottingham.
† Gives a convenient connection at Rolleston Junction to Nottingham.

		pm	pm	pm	pm	pm
Southwell	dep.	1.53	3.38	5.31	8.25	9.48
Rolleston Junction	arr.	1.58	3.43	5.36*	8.30*	9.53
Rolleston Junction	dep.	2.09			9.28	9.58
Newark	arr.	2.15			9.35	10.05

* Gives a convenient connection at Rolleston Junction to Lincoln.

FURTHER GROWTH IN THE COALFIELD, 1930 TO CLOSURE

		am	am	am	am	am	am
Newark	dep.	7.24		8.35	8.55		9.52
Rolleston Junction	arr.	7.31		8.42	9.02		9.59
	dep.	7.35	8.01*	8.43	9.08	9.37*	10.04
Southwell	arr.	7.40	8.06	8.48	9.13	9.42	10.09
		pm	pm	pm	pm	pm	pm
Newark	dep.	3.40	5.33		8.30		
Rolleston Junction	arr.	3.47	5.40		8.37		
Rolleston Junction	dep.	3.52		6.00*		8.52	10.02*
Southwell	arr.	3.57		6.05		8.57	10.07

* Convenient connection at Rolleston Junction from Nottingham.

Johnson 0-4-4T No. 1344 with 'The Paddy' at Southwell in this rare World War II scene on 17th December, 1941. Are those Christmas trees on the trolley on the station platform?   *H.C. Casserley*

The oil industry

Whilst coal had virtually been the *raison d'etre* for the continued existence of the line another element would soon appear which would give the line a further impetus in increasing the importance it had. When the surveys were carried out in connection with sinking a coal mine at Bilsthorpe there had been a suggestion that oil might also be found in the vicinity but at that point it would seem to be very much an aside and no further action was taken. Around the time of World War I, there was some exploration carried out but it was not followed through. However, during World War II, it was announced 'that a significant step had been taken in the search for oil in the area around Eakring, in Nottinghamshire'. The outcome was that Eakring No. 1 well was sunk and oil found at 1,975 ft. It was producing 100 tons of oil each week. This led to the decision to follow this up and it was anticipated that additional boring in the vicinity would result in

With a string of non-corridor coaches this excursion is probably taking its patrons the relatively short distance to Rolleston Junction station, located adjacent to Southwell racecourse. Headed by '4F' class No. 44394, still showing 'LMS' on the tender, the train has just called at Blidworth & Rainworth to pick up a few punters. *Jack Cupit*

Fowler '4F' class 0-6-0 No. 3983 of Mansfield shed is seen at Mansfield Colliery. *Jack Cupit*

further quantities. The area where this drilling took place was within easy reach of the line formerly known as the Mid-Nottinghamshire Joint Railway, with its facility of a connection to the Mansfield-Southwell line. The oil being brought to the surface would need to be taken to wherever it was needed and transport by rail would be necessary. Given that the country was at war and it was seen this oil would be an important element in making a contribution to the war effort, safe-guarding the details to prevent attracting the attention of any enemy action against it, resulted in information not being readily available.

The D'Arcy Exploration Co. continued to develop the oilfield in the Eakring area but gradually the output from the wells fell. When details became available it was disclosed that in 1943 in conjunction with the war effort some 235 tons each day were being resourced. By 1945 this had fallen dramatically and it was reported that as a result there were just nine wells left. Attempts to locate further oil resources in the immediate vicinity had failed. The company had decided to move on.

Post-World War II and nationalization

The war over, the service being run by 'The Paddy' continued and it still seemed to have a role to play, including travel facilities, for, amongst others, pupils attending Southwell Minster Grammar School. At that time the school was still situated next to Southwell Minster. The 1945 timetable read as follows:

Weekdays only   FSO SO

		am	am	am	am	am	am	am	pm	pm	pm	pm	pm	pm	pm
Southwell	dep.	6.40	7.27	7.50	8.30	8.55	9.55		1.10	2.10	4.10	5.10	5.35	6.05	6.50
Rolleston Jn	arr.	6.45	7.32	7.55	8.35	9.00	10.00		1.15	2.15	4.15	5.15	5.40	6.10	6.55
	dep.	6.46		7.57	8.37	9.43		11.03	1.23	2.17	4.56	5.23		6.15	6.58
Newark	arr.	6.53		8.05	8.44	9.51		11.11	1.31	2.24	5.03	5.30		6.22	7.05

                                                                                 SO SX SO

		am	am	am	am	am	am	pm	pm	pm	pm	pm	pm	pm	pm
Newark	dep.	7.07	7.27	7.54		8.54	9.54	1.10	1.14	1.24	4.10		5.34	5.55	
Rolleston Jn	arr.	7.14	7.35	8.02		9.03	10.02	1.18	1.23	1.33	4.18		5.43	6.03	
	dep.	7.15	7.40	8.05	8.40	9.05	10.05	1.25	2.20	2.20	4.20	5.25	5.48	6.20	7.00
Southwell	arr.	7.20	7.45	8.10	8.45	9.10	10.10	1.30	2.25	2.25	4.25	5.30	5.53	6.25	7.05

FSO – Fridays and Saturdays only, SO – Saturdays only, SX – Saturdays excepted.

With hostilities well over and new ways of thinking, in 1947 the Government of the day decided nationalization was a policy which would bring greater benefit to the country and this step included not only the railways but also the coal industry as well. The four companies that had been running the railways became British Railways (later British Rail) from 1st January, 1948 and the collieries became part of the National Coal Board. This step would have a considerable impact on how the railways were run and, not least, on the manner in which they served the east Nottinghamshire coalfield. Competition would no

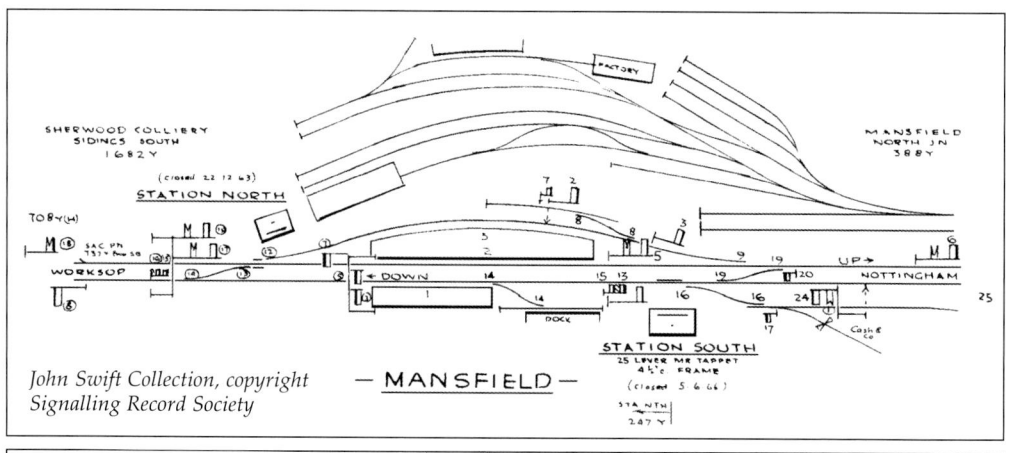
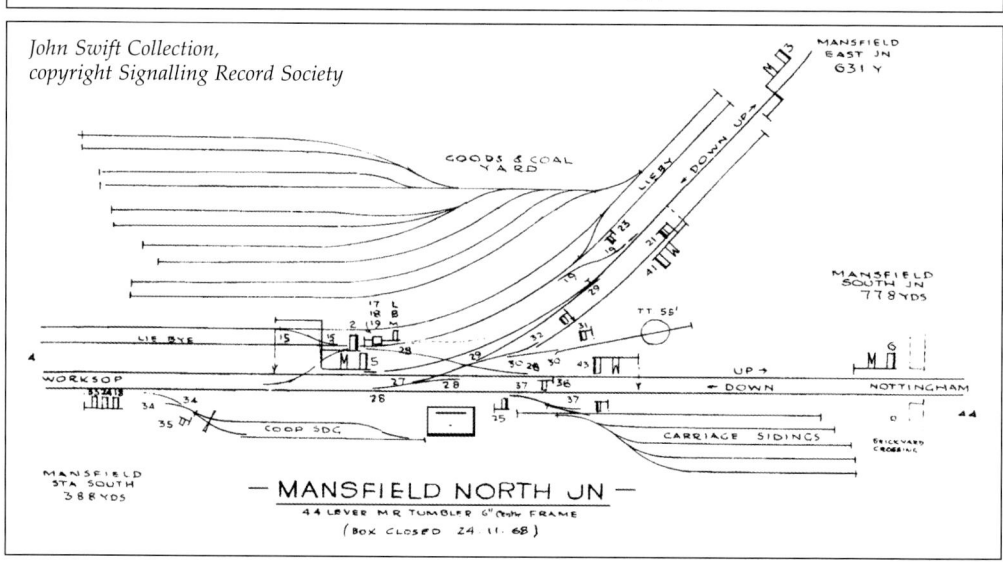
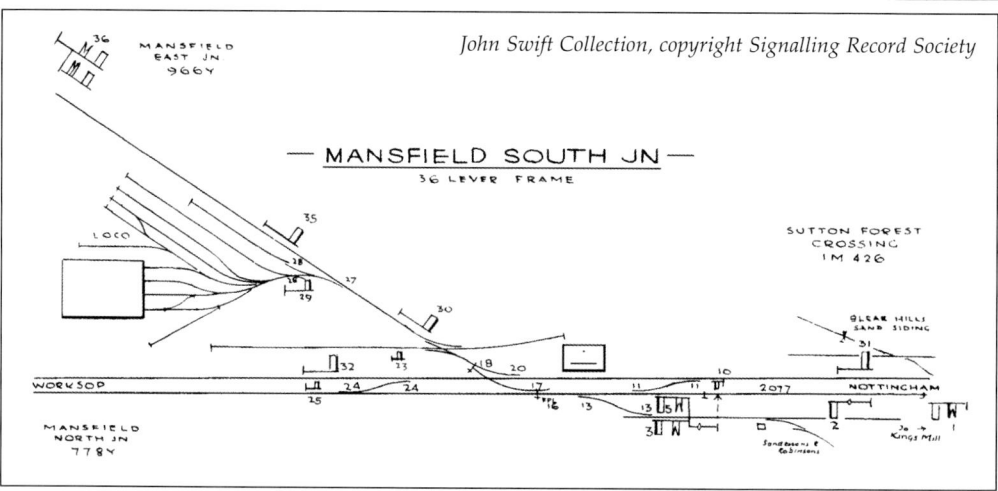

FURTHER GROWTH IN THE COALFIELD, 1930 TO CLOSURE

longer be involved and over a period of time changes, based to a large extent on economic factors, would be made. One outcome of this was that in 1948 the locomotive depot at Southwell was placed in the Eastern Region although this does not appear to have made any significant changes to the day-to-day running of the line.

In 1949 the working timetable for freight traffic showed a distinct predominance for the movement of coal. Details of this can be seen in the working timetable for the period which is reproduced on pages 72-75. Around this time there was only one general freight working each day on the line. This came from Newark, setting off at 1.24 pm on Mondays and at 1.35 pm on other weekdays, arriving at Southwell on both occasions 10 minutes later.

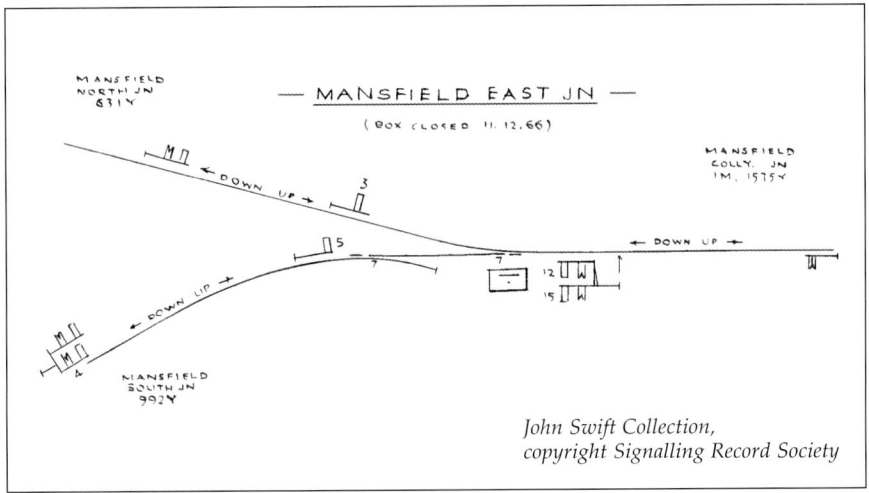

John Swift Collection, copyright Signalling Record Society

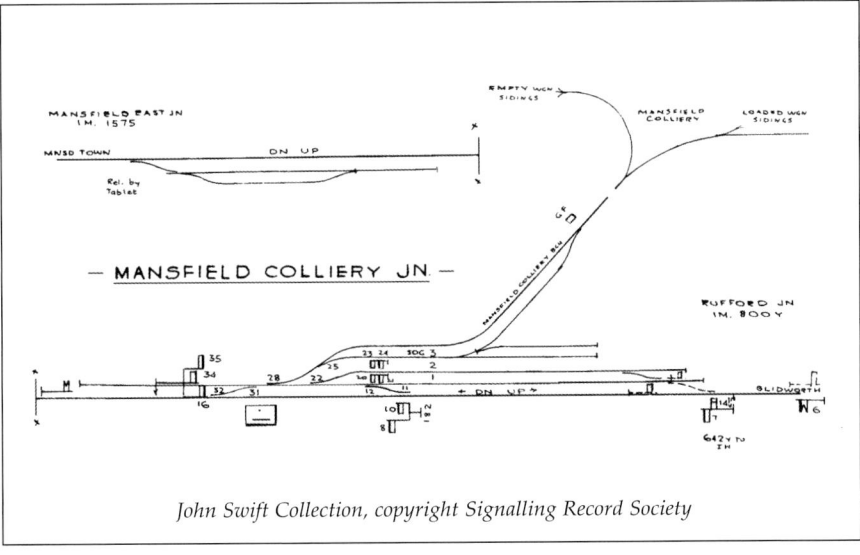

John Swift Collection, copyright Signalling Record Society

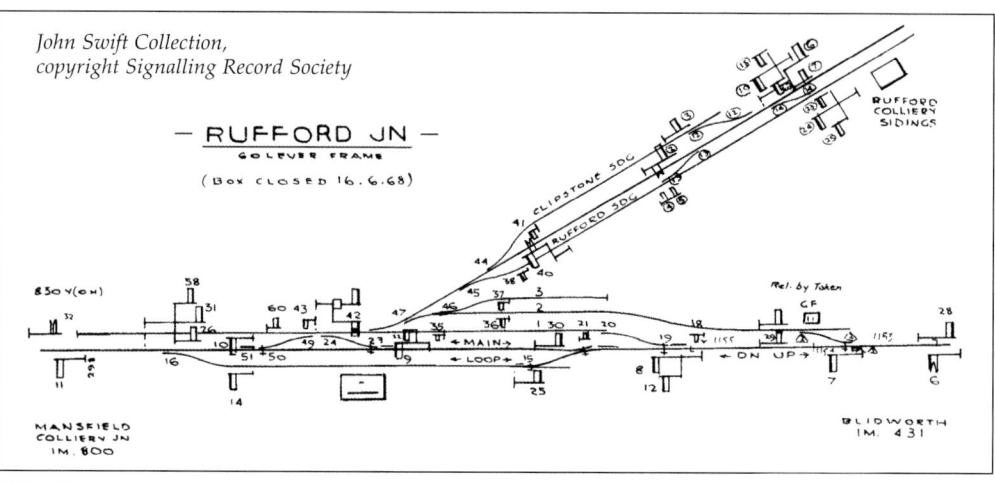

John Swift Collection, copyright Signalling Record Society

John Swift Collection, copyright Signalling Record Society

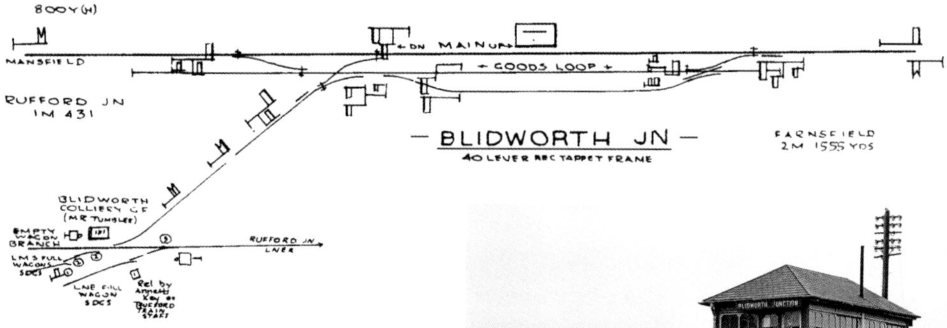

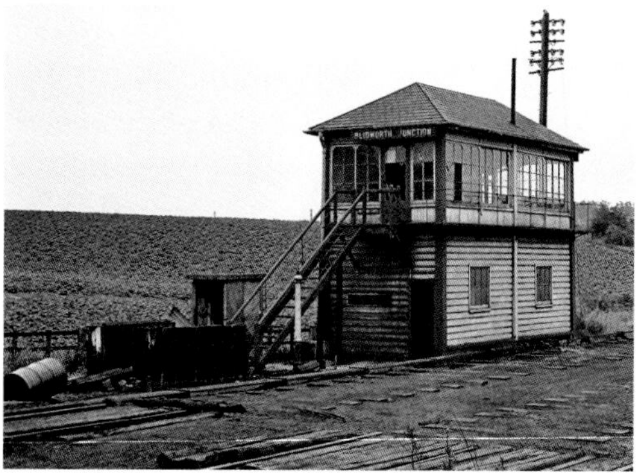

Blidworth Junction signal box in derelict condition on 24th June, 1967. Sleepers are still in place but the rails had recently been removed. *J.S. Hancock*

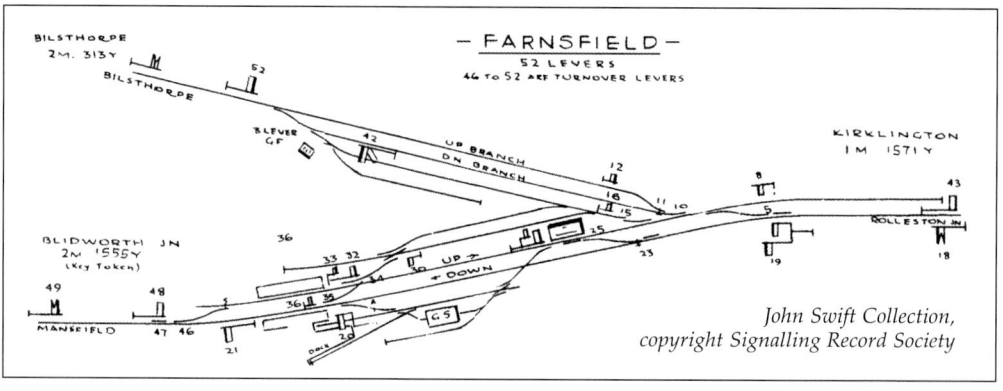

John Swift Collection, copyright Signalling Record Society

FURTHER GROWTH IN THE COALFIELD, 1930 TO CLOSURE

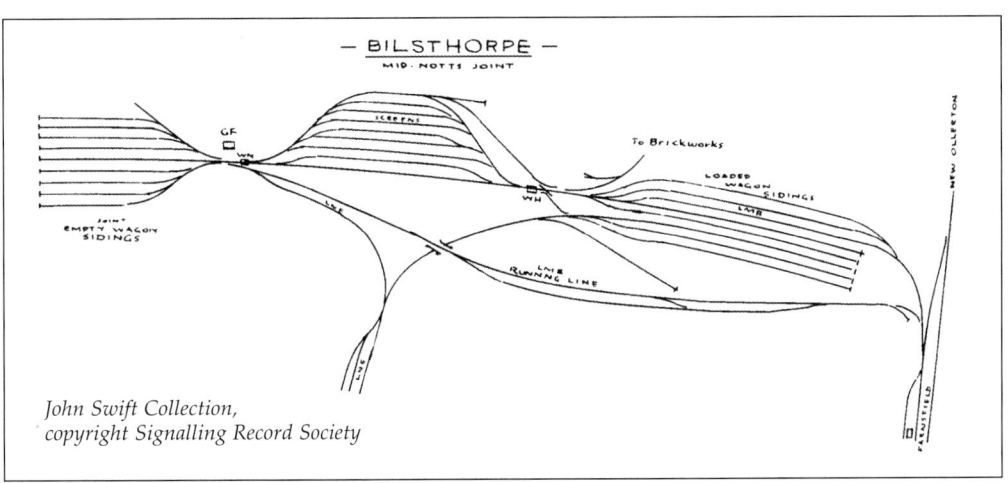

John Swift Collection,
copyright Signalling Record Society

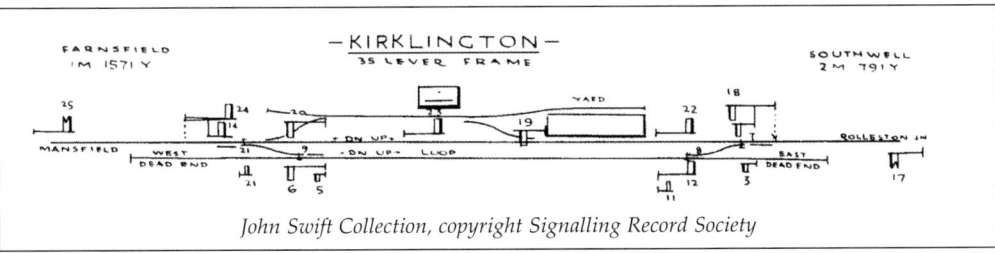

John Swift Collection, copyright Signalling Record Society

Kirklington signal box on 7th June, 1963.
Mick King

Southwell signal box in June 1962. *Mick King*

Upton Crossing signal box on 7th June, 1963. *Mick King*

FURTHER GROWTH IN THE COALFIELD, 1930 TO CLOSURE

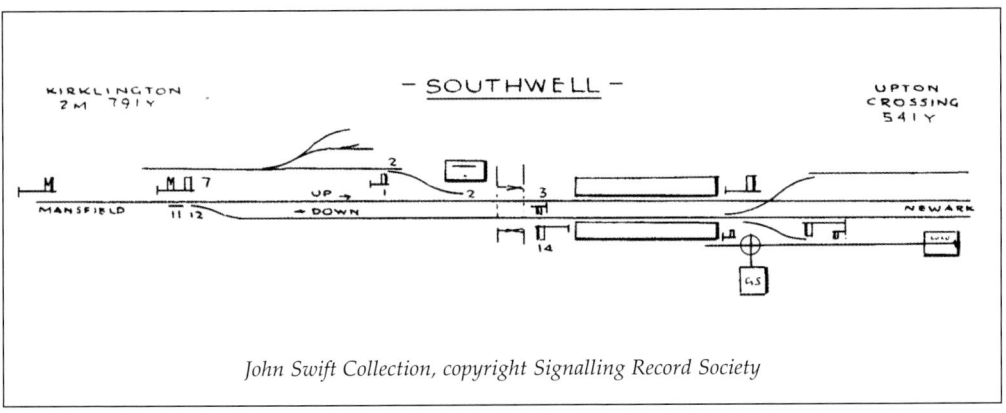

John Swift Collection, copyright Signalling Record Society

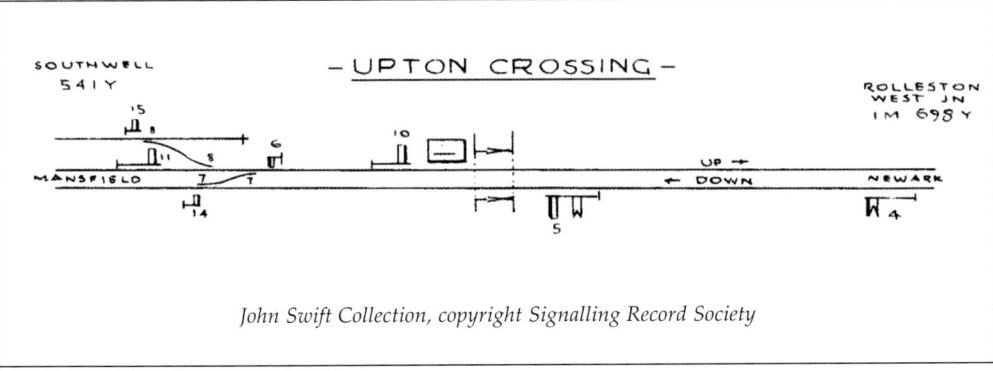

John Swift Collection, copyright Signalling Record Society

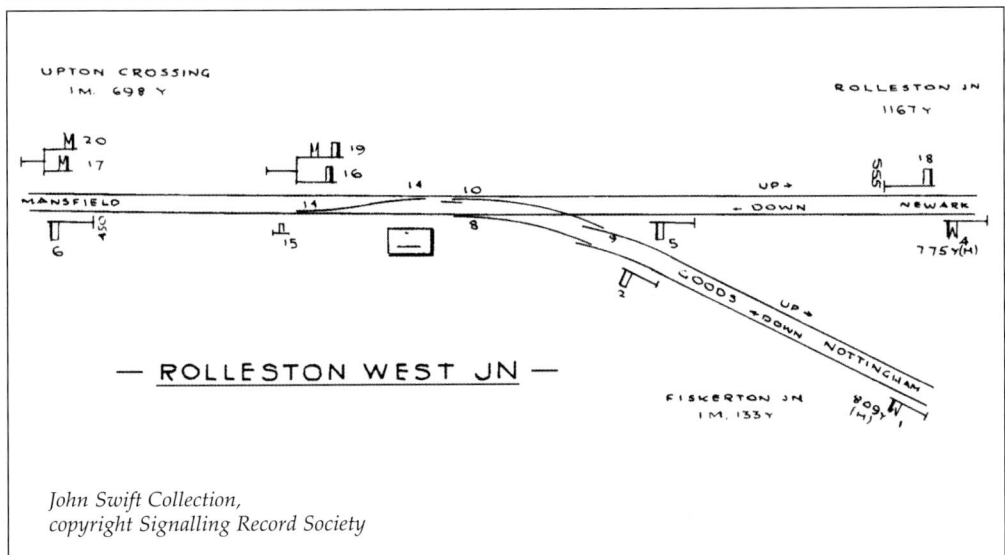

John Swift Collection,
copyright Signalling Record Society

MANSFIELD TO ROLLESTON JUNCTION.

Miles.		For continuation of trains from Junctions, see page	WEEKDAYS.	491	492	493	494	495	496	497	498	499	500	50	502
				1.0 a.m. Mineral (Empties) from Kirkby Sidings.	Mineral (Empties).	5.28 a.m. Engine and Brake from Kirkby Up Sidings.	6.40 a.m. E. & B. from Kirkby Down Sids.	Light Engine to Newark.	5.50 a.m. Empties from Kirkby Down Sidings.	Mineral to Beeston Sidings.	6.20 a.m. Mineral (Empties) from Kirkby Sidings.	Mineral (Empties).	Mineral.	Mineral.	8.25 a.m. E. & B. from Kirkby Up Sidings.
			Target No.	193	195	176		17	192		191	191	189	194	176
				MX		MX									MX
				a.m.	a.m.	a.m.	a.m.	a.m.	a.m.	a.m.	a.m.	a.m.	a.m.	a.m.	a.m.
0			MANSFIELD ....dep.	..	5†20	..	..	..	..	..	..	..	8† 6	8†30	..
¼		250	Mansfield North Junc.⊕..	..	..	..	..	..	..	..	..	..	..	..	..
	0	262	Mansfield S. Junc.⊕..	1*15	5*24	5*38	5*54	..	6* 8	..	6*36	..	8*10	8*34	8*39
¾	½		Mansfield East Junc.⊕..	1*18	5*28	5*41	5*57	..	6*10	..	6*39	..	8*15	8*38	8*48
			Mansfield Colliery⊕ arr.	..	..	5 50	..	..	..	..	..	..	8 23	..	..
2¼			Junc.............. dep.	1*25	5*36	..	6* 5	..	6*20	..	6*47	..	..	8*46	8*54
4	0		Rufford Junc. .....⊕ arr.	1 32	..	..	..	..	..	..	6 53	..	..	..	9 0
			dep.	..	5*42	..	6*12	..	6*26	..	..	7 8	..	8*53	..
	½		Rufford Colliery ⚲⊕....	..	..	..	..	..	6*29	..	..	7 15	..	..	..
			Clipstone Lie-by arr.	..	↑ Kings Mill.	..	..	(Newark Shunt Engine.)	..	..	..	..	..	..	..
	¾		dep.	..		..	..		..	..	..	..	..	..	..
	3¼		Clipstone Colliery ..arr.	..		..	..		6 48	..	..	..	..	..	..
5			Blidworth Junc. ⊕.......	..	5*53	..	6*18		..	..	..	..	..	9* 5	..
	0		Ollerton (Colliery LoadedWagonSids.)dep.	..	..	..	To work 7.4 a.m. to Beeston Sids.		..	..	..	..	..	↑ King's Mill.	..
	1		Ollerton (Colliery Empty Wagon Sids.)..	..		..			..	..	..	..			..
	5½		Bilsthorpe ....⚲⊕ arr.	..	Blidworth Jc. arr. 5*50, Blidworth Coll. arr. 6.0 a.m.	..			..	..	..	..	↑ Kings Mill	..	..
			dep.	..		..			..	..	..	..		..	..
7½	7½		Farnsfield........⊕ arr.	..		..	6 30	..	..	..	..	..		9 18	..
			dep.	..		..	..	..	..	7 4	..	..		..	..
9¾	—		Kirklington ......⊕......	..		..	..	..	..	7*16	..	..	..	Blidworth Junction arr. 9*2.	..
12			Southwell........⊕ arr.	..		..	..	..	..	..	..	..	..		..
			dep.	..		..	..	7 5	..	7*32	..	..	..		..
13½	0		Rolleston West Junc.	..	..	..	..	..	Signalled "Through Freight."	7 38	..	..	..		..
	1	307	Fiskerton Junc.........	..	..	..	..	..		7*48	..	..	..		..
14½	—	309	ROLLESTON JUNC. arr.	..	..	..	..	7 12		..	..	..	..		..

WEEKDAYS.	503	504	505	506	507	508		509	510	511	512	513	514	515
	Light Engine.	Engine and Brake.	Engine and Brake.	Engine and Brake.	Mineral to Wellingboro'.	Mineral to Beeston Sidings	Blidworth & R. arr. 10.46, dep. 10.55, Blidworth Jc. arr. 10.58, Kirklington arr. 11.56.	Stopping Freight to Newark.	Mineral (Empties).	Light Engine.	Mineral.	Mineral.	11.35 a.m. Mineral (Empties) from Kirkby Down Sidings.	Engine and Brake.
Target No.		192	191	191					191	157	168	194	195	191
	a.m.	a.m.	a.m.	a.m.	a.m.	a.m.		a.m.	a.m.	a.m.	a.m.	p.m.	a.m.	p.m.
MANSFIELD ....dep.	..	..	..	..	..	..		10 2	..	11† 0	11†20	..	..	..
Mansfield North Junc.⊕..	..	..	..	..	..	..		10* 5	..	..	11*24	..	..	..
Mansfield S. Junc. ⊕..	8†50	..	..	..	Blidworth Colliery (L.W.S.) dep. 9.40 a.m.	↑ Colliery L.W.S.		..	..	..		..	11L52	..
Mansfield East Junc.⊕..	8*55	..	..	..				10* 7	..	11* 5	11*28	Eakring Sidings arr. 12.35, dep. 12.50.	11*58	..
Mansfield Colliery⊕ arr.	..	..	..	..				10 15	..	..	11 55		..	..
Junc.............. dep.	9* 2	..	..	..				10 25	..	11*12	..		12* 6	..
Rufford Junc. .....⊕ arr.	..	..	..	..				10 32	..	11 20	..		..	..
dep.	9*10	8 45	8 53	9 55				10 41	10 55	..	..		12*12	12 25
Rufford Coll. ⚲⊕........	↑ Loco.	8*47	8 58	10 0				..	11 0	..	..		..	12 30
Clipstone Lie-by arr.		..	..	..	..			..	..	..	..		..	..
dep.		..	..	..	..			..	..	..	..		..	..
Clipstone Colliery ..arr.		9 0	..	..	..	Fiskerton Junc. dep. 11*33.		..	..	↑ Loco.	Standard Sand Co.'s Sidings arr. 11.32, dep. 11.50 a.m.	..	..	..
Blidworth Junc...⊕......	9*17	..	..	..	9*50			11 6	..			..	12*20	Light Engine to Newark.
Ollerton (Colliery LoadedWagonSids.)dep.	Blidworth Colly. L.W.S. arr. 9.20.	..	..	..	..			..	..	..		12 20	Blidworth Junc. dep. 12*23, Blidworth Coll. arr. 12.30 p.m.	
Ollerton (Colliery arr.		..	..	..	..			..	..	..		..		
Epty.WagonSds.) dep.		..	..	..	..			..	..	..		..		
Bilsthorpe ....⚲⊕ arr.		..	..	..	..	..		..	..	..	..	1 0		
dep.		..	..	..	..	10† 5		..	..	..	..	..		
Farnsfield........⊕ arr.		..	..	..	10 10	10 20		11 17	..	..	..	..		17
dep.	To work 9.40 a.m. to Wellingboro'.	..	..	..	10 20	10 40		11 47	..	..		..		
Kirklington ......⊕.....		..	..	..	10*32	10*56		12 5	..	..	↑ Yard.	..		p.m.
Southwell........⊕ arr.		..	..	..	..	..		12 13	..	..		..	..	..
dep.		..	..	..	10*42	11*10		1 0	..	..		..	..	2 0
Rolleston West Junc.		..	..	..	10 48	11 17		..	..	..		..	..	..
Fiskerton Junc.........		..	..	..	10 53	11*25		..	..	..		..	..	..
ROLLESTON JUNC. arr.		..	..	..	..	..		1 10	..	..		..	..	2 7

Working timetable September 1949.

MANSFIELD TO ROLLESTON JUNCTION.

WEEKDAYS.

	515a	516	517	518	519	520	521	522	523	524	525	526	527
	12.15 p.m. Mineral (Empties) from Kirkby Down Sds.	1.30 p.m. Mineral (Empties) from Kirkby Down Sds.	1.45 p.m. Mineral Empties from Sherwood Coll. Up Sids.	Light Engine	Mineral (Empties).	2.0 p.m. Mineral from Kirkby Down Sds.	Engine and Brake.	3.24 p.m. Mineral (Empties) from Kirkby Down Sds.	Engine and Brake.	3.52 p.m. Mineral (Empties) from Kirkby Down Sds.	Mineral S.E. Up Beeston to Storage Sidings.	5.20 p.m. Mineral (Empties) from Kirkby Down Sds.	Light Engine
Target No.	193	192	MW FO 158	193	190	192	191	192	190		190	157
	p.m.	p.m.	p.m.	p.m.		p.m.	p.m.	p.m.	p.m.	p.m.	p.m.	p.m.	p.m.
MANSFIELD ....dep.	..	..	..	2†5	..	..	..	..	..	..	..	..	5†50
Mansfield North Junc.⊕..	..	..	1*56	..	..	..	..	..	..	..	..	..	..
Mansfield S. Junc. ⊕..	12*29	1*45	..	..	..	2*15	..	3*40	..	5*36	..	5*36	..
Mansfield East Junc.⊕..	12*A38	1*48	1*59	2*10	..	2*18	..	3*43	..	5*43	..	5*43	5*55
Mansfield Colliery⊕ ⌠ arr.	..	..	..	..	..	2*25	..	..	..	..	..	..	..
Junc............⌡ dep.	12*49	1*55	2* 8	2*16	..	..	..	3*53	..	5*52	..	5*52	6* 2
Rufford Junc.....⊕ ⌠ arr.	..	2 3	..	2 22	..	..	..	..	..	..	..	6 0	6 10
⌡ dep.	12*55	2 15	2*14	†Loco.	3 0	..	4 15	4* 0	5 25	6* 0	..	..	..
Rufford Coll. ⊕..	12*58	2 20	..	..	3* 3	..	4 20	..	5 30	6* 3	..	..	..
Clipstone Lie-by ⌠ arr.	..	..	..	..	..	194	..	..	..	..	..	..	..
⌡ dep.	..	..	..	..	..	..	..	..	..	..	..	..	..
Clipstone Colliery..arr.	1 20	..	2*20	..	3 23	p.m.	..	..	..	6 20	..	..	†Loco.
Blidworth Junc...⊕......	..	..	..	Mineral.	..	..	..	4 36	..	..	..	..	..
Ollerton (Colliery LoadedWagonSids.)dep.	..	Mineral to Beeston Sidings.	..	..	..	4 20	..	Blidworth Jc, arr. 4.6, Colly. arr. 4.46	..	..	SUSPENDED.	..	..
Ollerton (Colliery ⌠ arr. Epty. Wagon Sids.) ⌡ dep.	..	..	..	..	..	..	..	..	..	..	..	..	..
Bilsthorpe ....⊕⌠ arr.	..	2† 0	..	MW FO p.m.	..	..	..	..	..	5†20	..	..	..
⌡ dep.	A—Arrive 12*.55 Attach 12.15 p.m. L.K. from Mansfield Loco (Target 157)	..	..	3 30	..	4*45	..	..	..	5 35	..	..	..
Farnsfield ....⊕ ⌠ arr.		2 15	2 32	3 44	..	5 0	..	..	..	6*20	..	..	..
⌡ dep.		2 45	..	..	..	..	..	..	..	6*32	..	..	..
Kirklington ....⊕..		2*57	..	..	..	..	..	..	..	..	..	..	..
Southwell......⊕ ⌠ arr.		..	..	..	..	..	..	..	..	..	..	..	..
⌡ dep.		3* 7	..	..	..	..	..	..	..	6*42	..	..	..
Rolleston West Junc. ...		3 14	..	..	..	..	..	..	..	6 48	..	..	..
Fiskerton Junc........		3 19	..	..	..	..	..	..	..	6 58	..	..	..
ROLLESTON JUNC. arr.		†Loop.	..	..	..	..	..	..	..	..	..	..	..

WEEKDAYS. | SUNDAYS.

	528	529	530	531	532	533	534	535	536	537	540	543	547	548
	Mineral.	Mineral.	Mineral (Empties).	7.0 p.m. Mineral (Empties) from Kirkby Sidings.	7.0 p.m. M. & B. from Kirkby Sids.	7.25 p.m. Mineral from Kirkby Down Sidings.	Engine and Brake.	Mineral to Wellingboro'.	Engine and Brake.		1.0 a.m. Mineral (Empties) from Kirkby Sidings.	Light Engine to Newark.	Light Engine to Newark.	
Target No.	191	178	194	173		193	190	173			193	17	17	
	p.m.	p.m.	p.m.	p.m.	p.m.	p.m.	p.m.	p.m.	p.m.		a.m.	a.m.	p.m.	
MANSFIELD ....dep.	..	6† 0	..	..	..	?	..	..	..		..	..	..	..
Mansfield North Junc.⊕..	..	6* 3	..	..	..	..	..	..	..		..	..	..	..
Mansfield S. Junc. ⊕..	Blidworth Colliery dep. 6.20 p.m.	..	6* 7	7*14	7*14	7*42	..	..	..		1*15	..	..	..
Mansfield East Junc.⊕..		..	..	7*16	7*16	7*45	..	..	..		1*18	..	..	..
Mansfield Colliery⊕ ⌠ arr.		..	..	..	..	7 53	..	..	..		..	..	..	..
Junc............⌡ dep.		..	..	7 25	7*25	..	..	..	..		1*25	..	..	..
Rufford Junc.....⊕ ⌠ arr.	†Yard.	..	..	7 35	7 35	..	8 15	8 55	9 25		1 32	..	..	..
⌡ dep.		..	..	7 45	..	..	8*18	..	9 30		..	..	..	..
Rufford Coll. ⊕..		..	..	7 50	..	..	..	..	..		..	..	..	..
Clipstone Lie-by ⌠ arr.		..	..	..	..	Coupled to Target 173	..	..	..		..	..	..	..
⌡ dep.		..	..	..	..	..	..	8 35	..		..	..	..	..
Clipstone Colliery..arr.		..	..	..	..	..	..	..	..		..	..	..	..
Blidworth Junc...⊕......	6*25	..	..	..	Engine and Brake column 532 coupled.	To work 8.59 p.m. Rufford Junc. to Wellingboro	..	9* 5	..		..	..	..	..
Ollerton (Colliery LoadedWagonSids.)dep.	..	Standard Sand Co.'s Sidings arr. 6.13 p.m.	..	..		..	..	..	..		..	..	..	..
Ollerton (Colliery ⌠ arr. Empty Wagon Sids.) ⌡ dep.	..	..	..	..		..	..	..	..		..	..	..	..
Bilsthorpe ....⊕⌠ arr.	..	..	..	7 0		..	..	..	..		..	..	..	..
⌡ dep.	..	..	..	7 15		..	..	..	..		..	..	..	..
Farnsfield ....⊕ ⌠ arr.	6 38	..	..	..		..	..	9*17	..		..	Newark Shunt Engine.	..	..
⌡ dep.	..	..	..	..		..	..	9*26	..		..	..	..	..
Kirklington ....⊕..	..	..	..	..		..	..	9*36	..		8 0	12 30	..	..
Southwell......⊕ ⌠ arr.	..	..	..	..		..	..	9 42	..		..	..	..	..
⌡ dep.	..	..	..	..		..	..	9*48	..		..	..	..	..
Rolleston West Junc. ...	..	..	..	..		..	..	..	..		8 6	12 36	..	..
Fiskerton Junc........	..	..	..	..		..	..	..	..		..	..	..	..
ROLLESTON JUNC. arr.	..	..	..	..		..	..	..	..		..	..	..	..

Working timetable September 1949.

ROLLESTON JUNCTION TO MANSFIELD.

WEEKDAYS.

Miles.	For continuation of trains from junc. see page		550	551	552	553	554		555	556	557	558	559	560	561
			Light Engine.	Mineral to Kirkby Up Sidings.	Mineral to Kirkby Up Sidings.		Mineral.	8.16 a.m. Kirkby	7.35 a.m. Empties from Newark.	Mineral.	Mineral to Kirkby Up Sidings.	Mineral.	Mineral to Kirkby Up Sidings.	Mineral.	Mineral.
		Target No.	157	193	176		192			191	195	191		176	192	194
			MX	MX										MX		
			a.m.	a.m.	a.m.	..	a.m.	..	a.m.	a.m.	a.m.	a.m.	a.m.	a.m.	a.m.	a.m.
0	307	ROLLESTON JUNC. dep.	..	..	..	..	..	..	7 47	..	..	..	..	..	..	..
0	309	Fiskerton Junc.........	..	..	..	..	..			..	..	..	..	..	..	..
1	1	Rolleston West Junc.....	..	..	..	..	..			..	..	..	..	..	..	..
2¼	—	Southwell ⊕ { arr.	..	..	..	..	..			..	..	..	..	..	..	..
		{ dep.	..	..	..	..	..			..	..	..	..	..	..	..
4¾		Kirklington ⊕	..	..	..	..	..		7*57	..	..	..	..	..	..	..
6¼	0	Farnsfield ⊕ { arr.	..	..	..	..	..		8* 7	..	..	..	..	..	..	..
		{ dep.	..	..	..	..	..			..	..	..	..	..	9 45	..
	2	Bilsthorpe ⊕ { arr.	..	..	..	..	..		8*15	..	..	..	..	..	10 0	..
		{ dep.	..	..	..	..	..		8‡35	..	..	..	..	..	10 10	..
		Ollerton (Colliery	..	..	..	..	..			..	..	..	..	..	..	..
6¾		EmptyWag.Sids.) { dep.	..	..	..	..	..			..	..	..	..	..	..	..
7½		Ollerton (Colliery LoadedWagonSids.) arr.	..	..	..	..	..			..	..	..	..	..	..	..
9½	0	Blidworth Junc...⊕.....	..	..	..	..	..			..	8 38	..	..	..	10 55	..
	2¼	Clipstone Colliery..dep.	..	..	..	..	7 50			..	..	..	..	10 0	..	..
		Clipstone Lie-by { arr.	† Loco.	..	..	..	..			..	..	..	..	..	..	
		{ dep.	..	..	..	..	..			..	..	..	..	..	..	Baking Sidings arr. 10.30, dep.10.40.
10½	2¾	Rufford Coll..⊕⊕..dep.	..	..	..	..	8* 5			8 30	..	9 30	..	10*20	..	
	3½	Rufford Junc.....⊕ { arr.	..	..	..	..	8 10			8 35	8 53	9 35	..	10 25	..	
		{ dep.	12 1	2 35	..	..	..			9 0	..	..	9 45	..	..	
12¼		Mansfield Colliery { arr.															
		Junc...........⊕ { dep.	12* 8	2*42	6 50	..	..			9* 7	..	9*52	..	..	..	
13¾	0	Mansfield East Junc. ⊕	12*15	2*50	6*57	..	..			9*15	..	10* 0	..	..	..	
		Mansfield South Junc..........⊕	12‡20	2*56	7* 0	..	..			9*19	..	10* 4	..	..	..	
14¼	½250	Mansfield North Junc.⊕	..	..	..	..	..			..	..	..	..	..	..	
14¾	262	MANSFIELD ......arr.	..	..	..	..	..			..	..	..	..	..	..	

WEEKDAYS.

	562	563	564	565	566	567	568	569	570	571	572	573	574	575
	Mineral.	Mineral to Kirkby Up Sidings.	Mineral.	10.20a.m. Mln. (N'tlon) from Lenton S. Ju. (N.W.F.S.).	Engine and Brake.	Mineral to Kirkby Side.	2.24 p.m. F'ght from Newark.	1.35 p.m. F'ght from Newark.	Mineral.	Mineral.	Mineral to Elmton & C.	Mineral Empties.	Mineral.	Mineral to Kirkby Up Sidings.
Target No.	191	192	191		168	191	17	17	194	193	195		192	190
							MQ	MX				MW FO		
	a.m.	a.m.	noon	a.m.	..	p.m.	p.m.	p.m.	p.m.	p.m.	p.m.	p.m.	p.m.	p.m.
ROLLESTON JUNC. dep.	..	..	..	..	..	..	1 34	1 45	..	..	..	..	..	..
Fiskerton Junc.........	..	..	..	11 40	..	..	..	..	..	..	..	..	..	..
Rolleston West Junc.....	..	..	..	11 43	..	..	..	..	..	..	..	..	..	..
Southwell ⊕ { arr.	..	..	..	11 48	..	..	1 44	1 55	..	..	..	..	..	..
{ dep.	..	..	..	11 53	..	..	..	..	..	..	..	..	..	..
Kirklington ⊕	..	..	..	12* 3	..	..	..	..	..	..	..	..	..	..
Farnsfield ⊕ { arr.	..	..	..	12*12	..	..	..	..	..	..	..	2 50	..	..
{ dep.	..	..	..	12‡27	..	..	..	..	..	..	..	3 7	..	..
Bilsthorpe ⊕ { arr.	..	..	..	..	..	..	..	..	2 0	..	..	..	..	..
{ dep.	..	..	..	..	..	..	..	..	..	..	..	..	..	..
Ollerton (Colliery { arr.	..	..	..	..	..	..	..	..	..	..	..	..	..	..
EmptyWag.Sids.) { dep.	..	..	..	..	..	..	..	..	..	..	..	..	..	..
Ollerton (Colliery LoadedWagonSids.) arr.	..	..	..	..	..	..	..	..	2 25	..	..	..	..	..
Blidworth Junc.........	..	..	..	..	..	..	..	..	..	..	2 45	..	..	..
Clipstone Colliery..dep.	..	..	..	..	..	..	..	..	..	2 15	..	..	..	..
Clipstone Lie-by { arr.	..	..	..	† Loop	..	..	..	..	..	..	..	..	..	..
{ dep.	..	..	..	..	..	..	..	..	..	..	..	..	..	..
Rufford Coll..⊕..dep.	10 30	..	12 0	When required works Empties to Blisthorpe Colly. E.W.S.	1 10	..	..	..	2*32	..	..	3 40	..	
Rufford Junc.....⊕ { arr.	10 35	..	12 5		† Yard.	..	..	..	2 36	2 50	..	3 45	..	
{ dep.	..	10 50	..		1*15	..	..	..	..	3* 8	..	..	..	
Mansfield Colliery { arr.														
Junc........... { dep.	..	10*57	..		12 22	1*22	..	..	3*15	..	..	3 25	..	
Mansfield East Junc. ⊕	..	11* 5	..		12*30	1*32	..	..	3*22	..	..	3*35	..	
Mansfield South Junc..........⊕	..	11* 8	..		1*36	..	..	..	..	..	..	3*38	..	
Mansfield North Junc.⊕	..	..	..		12*34	..	..	..	..	3 28	..	..	..	
MANSFIELD .....arr.	..	..	..		12‡38	..	..	..	..	..	..	..	..	

Working timetable September 1949.

ROLLESTON JUNCTION TO MANSFIELD.

WEEKDAYS.

	576	577	578	579	580	581	582	583	584	585	586	587	588
	E.P. to Carlisle (Canal Yard).	Mineral to Kirkby Up Sidings.	Mineral.	2.0 p.m. Min. (Empties) from Beeston Down Side.	2.40 p.m Stoy'r's Freight from Newark.	Mineral.	Mineral to Kirkby Up Sidings.	Mineral to Kirkby Up Sidings.	Engine and Brake.	Mineral.	Mineral.	Mineral.	Mineral to Kirkby Up Sidings.
Target No.	MW FO	193	192			194	178	192	191	190	189	194	191
	p.m.	p.m.	p.m.	p.m.	p.m.	p.m.	p.m.	p.m.	p.m.	p.m.	p.m.	p.m.	p.m.
ROLLESTON JUNC. dep.	..	..	..	..	2 52	..	..	..	..	..	..	..	..
Fiskerton Junc.......f.	..	..	..	3 18		..	..	..	..	..	..	..	..
Rolleston West Junc.....	..	..	..	3 21		..	..	..	..	..	..	..	..
Southwell ⊕ { arr.	..	..	..		3 2	..			..	..	†Yard.	†Down Lie-by.	..
{ dep.	..	..	..	3*29	3 45	..		Standard Sand Co.'s Sidings dep. 6.45 p.m.	..	..			..
Kirklington ⊕.........	..	..	..	3*38	4 10	..			..	..			..
Farnsfield ⊕ { arr.	..	..	..		4 20	..			..	..			..
{ dep.	4 22	..	..	3*45	4 40	5 38			7 15	..		7 45	..
Bilsthorpe ..✧⊕ { arr.	..	..	..	4† 5		5 53			..	..			..
Ollerton (Colliery { arr.	..	..	..			..			..	..			..
EmptyWag.Sids.) { dep.	..	..	..			..			..	..			..
Ollerton (Colliery LoadedWagonSids.)arr.	..	..	..			..			..	..			..
Blidworth Junc...⊕....	4*38	..	..	5 2		..			7*25	..		7*55	..
Clipstone Colliery..dep.	..	4 15	..			192			..	7 20			..
Clipstone Lie-by { arr.	..	..	..			p.m.			..				..
{ dep.	..	4*30	4 50			6 5			..	7*40			..
Rufford Coll....✧⊕.....	..	4 35	4 55			6 10			7 30	7 45			..
Rufford Junc. ⊕ { arr.	..							6 46				8* 0	8 10
{ dep.	4*45	5 0			5*23								
Mansfield Colliery { arr.											7 55	8* 7	8*20
Junc. ⊕ { dep.	4*52	5* 8			5*30			6*54					
Mansfield East Junc.⊕..	5* 0	5*18			5*40		6*50	7* 4			8* 3	8*15	8*32
Mansfield South Junc. ⊕..........		5*21					6*53	7*11					8*34
Mansfield North Junc.⊕..	5* 5				5*46						8* 8	8†20	
MANSFIELD ....arr.					5 50						8†12		

WEEKDAYS. / SUNDAYS.

	589	590	591	592	593	594	595	596	597	602	603	607	608	609	610
	Light Engine.	Mineral to Kirkby Up Sidings.	Mineral to Kirkby Up Sidings.	Mineral.	9.2 p.m. L.E. from Newark.	Mineral to Kirkby Up Sidings.	Mineral.	Mineral.	Mineral to Kirkby Up Sidings.	Light Engine.	Mineral to Kirkby Up Sidings.		12.10 p.m. L.E. from Newark.	4.15 p.m. L.E. from Newark.	Mineral.
Target No.	158	190	193	173	17	190	173		173	157	193		17	17	
	p.m.	p.m.	p.m.	p.m.	p.m.	p.m.	p.m.		p.m.	a.m.	a.m.		p.m.	p.m.	
ROLLESTON JUNC. dep.	..	..	..	..	9 12	..	..	..	..	..	..	..	12 19	4 25	..
Fiskerton Junc...........	..	..	..			..		..	..	..	..	..			..
Rolleston West Junc.....	..	..	..			..		..	..	..	..	..			..
Southwell ⊕ { arr.	†Loco.	..	..		9 17	..		..	..	..	..	..	12 25	4 30	..
{ dep.		..	..			..		..	..	..	..	..			..
Kirklington ⊕..........	†	..	..			..		..	..	..	..	..	†Newark Shunt Engine.		..
Farnsfield ⊕ { arr.		..	..			..		..	..	..	..	..			..
{ dep.		..	..	SUSPENDED.		..	Mineral.	..	..	..	..	..			..
Bilsthorpe ..✧⊕ { arr.		..	..			..		..	..	..	..	..			..
Ollerton (Colliery { arr.		..	..			..		..	..	..	..	..			..
EmptyWag.Sids.) { dep.		..	..			..		..	..	..	..	..			..
Ollerton (Colliery LoadedWagonSids.)arr.		..	..		189	..		..	..	..	..	..			..
Blidworth Junc...⊕....	..	..	..		p.m.	..		..	..	..	..	†Loco.			..
Clipstone Colliery..dep.	..	..	..			..	9 10	..	..	..	..				..
Clipstone Lie-by { arr.	..	..	..			..		..	..	..	..				..
{ dep.	..	..	..		9 0	9*30	9 50	..	..	..	..				..
Rufford Coll...✧⊕ dep.	..	..	..	SUSPENDED.	9 5	9 35	9 55	..	..	..	..				..
Rufford Junc.....⊕ { arr.	8 25	8 35				10 45		..	11 15	12 1	2 35				..
{ dep.					†Yard.										
Mansfield Colliery { arr.															
Junc. ⊕ { dep.	8*33	8*43	9 5		10 10	10*52		..	11*22	12* 8	2*42				..
Mansfield East Junc. ⊕.	8*40	8*53	9*14		10*18	11* 2		..	11*32	12*15	2*50				..
Mansfield South Junc. ⊕.............	8†45	9* 0	9*20			11* 9		..	11*38	12†20	2*56				..
Mansfield North Junc.⊕..					10*22			..							..
MANSFIELD........arr.					10†26			..							..

Derby, September, 1949.

L. P. BALL, Divisional Operating Superintendent.

Working timetable September 1949.

THE MANSFIELD-SOUTHWELL-ROLLESTON RAILWAY

Class '3F' No. 43494 heads a short goods train near one of several sand quarries just to the east of the town. Mansfield sand has been (and remains) a staple product of the area since at least the 1700s, used for building and especially moulding. *Jack Cupit*

Manning, Wardle & Co. Ltd 0-4-0ST *Empress* worked in the sand quarry located to the east of Mansfield East Junction. The Ordnance Survey map reproduced on page 42 shows this locomotive's engine shed and the lines which it worked on. *Jack Cupit*

FURTHER GROWTH IN THE COALFIELD, 1930 TO CLOSURE

The end of 'The Paddy'

'The Paddy' still had a place in the operation of the line with the pattern of services much the same as that following the war. On each Monday it was still possible to see it travelling empty to and from Nottingham. The purpose was a weekly change of stock and it included cleaning the trailer unit.

There was another change in a station name on 11th August, 1952 when 'Mansfield' became 'Mansfield Town'. What may have appeared to be a further sign that times were changing was the closure of the Southwell depot on 10th January, 1955. This resulted in the locomotive being transferred to Newark shed. The coach continued to be kept at Southwell which meant the locomotive travelled light to and from Newark at the beginning and end of the day. Occasionally, in addition to the race specials, there were other types of excursions to be seen on the line, especially in the summer. One such was observed on 21st July, 1957 bound for Skegness.

In January 1959, Newark shed closed and so the locomotive for 'The Paddy' was transferred to Lincoln. However, with the subsequent closure of the Midland shed at Lincoln, the only shed available was the former GNR one. This was not the most satisfactory of arrangements given the considerable distance from Lincoln to Southwell and the time involved for the light engine. Together with this it was alleged that passenger numbers were falling. The outlook did not appear to be good and perhaps it was not surprising when the decision was made, now based on the grounds of economy, that the service be withdrawn. The announcement, in March, did not prove to be one which was readily accepted and a decision was made to oppose the plan. In April there was a protest by the Transport Users' Consultative Committee. This proved to be of no avail and so with what would seem quite a lot of sentiment and cause for regret, 'The Paddy' was withdrawn in June. It was noted in the press that 'a large number chose to travel on the last service' on 13th June, 1959.

Later a local pub would be named 'The Final Whistle' in memory of what had been described as 'a much loved service'.

Standard motive power over many years for 'The Paddy' were 0-4-4Ts built for the Midland Railway. Here we see 1886-built No. 1324 at Southwell, still bearing LMS livery on 21st June, 1952. *Jack Cupit*

No. 58056 leaving Southwell for Rolleston Junction on 19th April, 1952. This Johnson engine, with its 5 ft 4 in. driving wheels, was ideal for push-pull working on the branch.   *Jack Cupit*

A three-quarter rear view of No. 58085 and its train at Southwell on 3rd September, 1955 which illustrates well the push-pull carriage. Held by the signal in a quiet moment between trips, the fireman appears to be in serious conversation with a young lad.   *Jack Cupit*

No. 58065 looks ready for action outside Southwell shed in July 1958. *P.H. Groom*

In this mid-1950s view No. 58065 stands next to the water column at Southwell shed surrounded by piles of ash and clinker. *R.S. Carpenter Collection*

No. 58086, with its safety valves blowing off, stands in the platform at Southwell *circa* April 1958.
Stephenson Locomotive Society

Ex-MR '2228' class 0-4-4T No. 58085 at Rolleston Junction on 3rd September, 1955 with 'The Paddy'.
Jack Cupit

A mid-1950s view of ex-Midland Railway '1833' class 0-4-4T No. 58065 with 'The Paddy' at Rolleston Junction.
Jack Cupit

On 2nd September, 1955 ex-Great Northern Railway 0-6-0 (LNER 'J6') No. 64245 is seen standing at Southwell waiting to leave with the 2.00 pm for Rolleston Junction. The station master's house, seen in the background, is a Grade II-listed building and has been sympathetically renovated and as 'Southwell Station House' offers bed and breakfast accommodation.

H.C. Casserley

A view of 'A5' class 4-6-2T No. 69808 leaving Southwell station on 9th May, 1959, just a month before withdrawal of 'The Paddy'. Dominating the skyline is Caudwell's flour mill. The mill remained in use until 1977 and has since been converted into apartments. *Jack Cupit*

Fowler '4F' class No. 44470 looks a little care-worn but is good enough to be trusted with an excursion near Blidworth Junction.
Jack Cupit

Ex- LMS Hughes/Fowler 'Crab' 2-6-0 No. 42768 with its tender well stacked with decent coal, runs through Blidworth & Rainworth station tender-first with (presumably) an excursion. The train is classed express according to the lamps but had it been an ordinary passenger train where would you put the lamp on the back of a Fowler tender?
Jack Cupit

On 31st July, 1957 an excursion to Cleethorpes which started from Teversal Manor station has taken the curve from Mansfield North to Mansfield East Junction with Hughes/Fowler 'Crab' 2-6-0 No. 42797 in charge. *Jack Cupit*

Excursion trains to Rolleston Junction for race meetings at Southwell racecourse generated much income for the railway over the years. This handbill promotes two trains, one from Hucknall and the other from Worksop, for the race meeting held on 16th April, 1960. *W. Taylor Collection*

Rushing past Blidworth Colliery Junction (LMS) is 'Crab' No. 42768, borrowed from Rowsley shed, with a races special to Rolleston Junction on 28th March, 1959. This view was taken from the LNER Blidworth Colliery branch which passed above the Southwell line. *Jack Cupit*

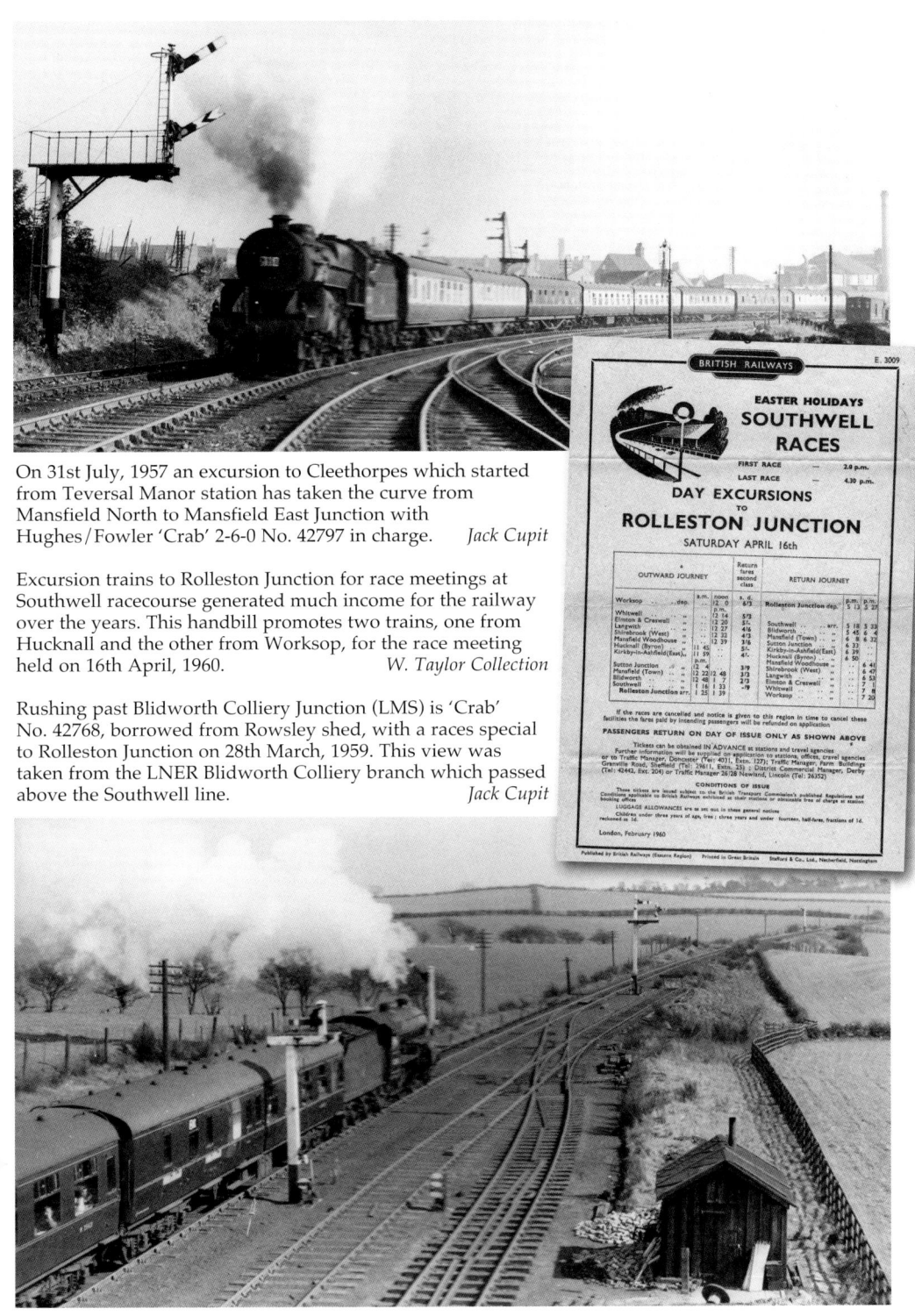

A Midland Railway map showing Mansfield station and the triangular junction to the south of it which gave access to the Southwell line.

FURTHER GROWTH IN THE COALFIELD, 1930 TO CLOSURE 85

A post-nationalization view of the station approach of Mansfield's former Midland Railway station, by now bearing the name 'Mansfield Town'. *Heyday Publishing*

Mansfield station, looking south beneath the trainshed, along Platform 2 in May 1953.
Douglas Thompson

In June 1955, at the south end of Mansfield station we see '3F' class 0-6-0 No. 43727 and an unidentified '8F' class 2-8-0 with a coal train bound for Toton yard. *Douglas Thompson*

A view from the 12.23pm Saturdays-only train arriving at Platform 1 at Mansfield Town station on 5th May, 1962. The locomotive is Fairburn 2-6-4T No. 42232. Platforms 1 and 2 were sheltered by the trainshed. Platform 3, to the right, was from where, at one time, regular passenger trains would have departed for Southwell. The goods shed can be seen in the background.

Milepost 92½

'4F' class 0-6-0 No. 44268 is seen with a Nottingham-bound goods train as it passes Mansfield North Junction signal box on 28th April, 1962. The Southwell line is to the right. *Jack Cupit*

The signalman at Mansfield North Junction receives the Southwell line tablet from the crew of a Stanier '8F' class 2-8-0 on 29th September, 1962. *W. Taylor*

Stanier '3MT' class 2-6-2T No. 40079 passes Mansfield South Junction with an unusual working to Ambergate where a connection with an express service was advertised, the details of which are unknown. The single line going off right is to Mansfield East Junction on the Southwell line, but it also serves as the exit from Mansfield shed seen in the distance. *Jack Cupit*

A 1950s view of Mansfield engine shed with a varied line up of motive power. Outside the shed, from left to right, are Hughes/Fowler 'Crab' 2-6-0 No. 42760, an unidentified Fowler '4F' 0-6-0 centre, and Whitelegg 4-4-2T No. 41943 that had originally been intended for work on the former London, Tilbury & Southend Railway. Peering out from within the shed on the right is Stanier '8F' class 2-8-0 No. 48156. *Provenance Unknown*

FURTHER GROWTH IN THE COALFIELD, 1930 TO CLOSURE

Mansfield-allocated '8F' class 2-8-0 No. 48541 heads a train of tanks having just passed Mansfield East Junction on 23rd April, 1957. The tanks are filled with crude oil from the first British inland oilfield at Eakring which started production during World War II and are destined for a refinery at Pumpherston near Edinburgh. The train joined the Southwell line at Farnsfield from the Mid-Nottinghamshire Joint line and will proceed via Mansfield North Junction, Clowne and Rotherham to York. On the right (just visible) are wagons in the first of three sand sidings adjacent to the line. To the left, the goods yard of the Mansfield Railway (worked by the Great Central) shows plenty of traffic to deal with. *Jack Cupit*

Mansfield East Junction is where the lines from Mansfield North and South junctions respectively met each other and where we see Kirkby shed's '8F' class 2-8-0 No. 48395 heading east on the single line. *Jack Cupit*

A view along the platform at Farnsfield looking towards Mansfield. Taken on 7th June, 1963, it had been more than 30 years since regular timetabled trains had called here. *Mick King*

A general view of a somewhat down-at-heel Farnsfield station looking east towards the substantial goods shed. *Douglas Thompson*

FURTHER GROWTH IN THE COALFIELD, 1930 TO CLOSURE

The station buildings at Southwell in May 1963 in a view looking towards Rolleston. By this date the locomotive shed had been demolished. Upton crossing gates and signal box can be seen in the distance. *V.R. Webster/Kidderminster Railway Museum*

Southwell station viewed from the road. The ultimate nemesis of the passenger service on the Southwell line, a local service bus, can be seen far right. *W. Taylor Collection*

A view looking east from Southwell station on 31st May, 1958. Notice the cattle dock on the right, and the engine shed in the distance. *R.S. Carpenter Collection*

Station staff pose on the main line platform at Rolleston in this view looking towards Newark.
Douglas Thompson

FURTHER GROWTH IN THE COALFIELD, 1930 TO CLOSURE

The 1960s

It was during 1964 that with the growth of goods being transported more and more by road with the advantage of what became known as 'the once handled principle' for delivery systems, trade for the service of general goods on many local railways became uneconomical. This was especially so in rural areas where the quantities involved were often not very great. The outcome was a gradual withdrawal and this turned out to be the case as far as the intermediate stations along the Mansfield-Southwell line were concerned. The first to lose this facility was Farnsfield on 26th April, 1964, the next being Kirklington on 25th May and then Southwell on 7th December. This just left Blidworth and Rainworth and the service was withdrawn on 1st February, 1965.

Then came a rationalization programme. British Rail began the procedure to 'single service' the collieries. Inevitably for those in the east Nottinghamshire coalfield this would have an impact on the Mansfield-Southwell line in terms of its usefulness. By 1968 this rationalization became more drastic.

The decision was made to truncate the Mansfield-Southwell line and to close the section from Farnsfield eastwards. This left the section from the junction to Rufford and Clipstone collieries open and the section of the line which remained would continue to serve in part these collieries with coal being moved through Mansfield. This practice was to continue for some years.

Within about 12 months the track on this redundant section of the line would be taken up. There followed a development which would eventually use the trackbed in an imaginative and beneficial way.

With the spoil heap of Crown Farm Colliery to the right two unidentified '8F' class 2-8-0s are seen hard at work with their full load. *Booklaw Publications*

A double-headed train hauled by a '4F' class 0-6-0 and '8F' class 2-8-0 are seen leaving Mansfield Colliery, its modern washing plant forms the backdrop on 2nd May, 1959. *Jack Cupit*

It is 28th January, 1959 and Mansfield Colliery Junction has lost its Midland Railway signal arms which have been replaced with upper quadrant types. A shunter, complete with pole, is in charge of movements on the colliery sidings line where '8F' class 2-8-0s Nos. 48100 and 48528 provide the motive power. Two locomotives for the Mansfield Colliery branch was normal.
Jack Cupit

FURTHER GROWTH IN THE COALFIELD, 1930 TO CLOSURE

A pair of '8F' 2-8-0s, the leading one being No. 48100, are seen on the climb out of Mansfield Colliery with about 28 unbraked wagons mostly of 16 tons capacity. The familiar outline of Crown Farm's tip confirms the location. *Jack Cupit*

A snowy scene with Stanier '8F' class 2-8-0 No. 48100 next to Rufford Colliery Sidings signal box with a brake van on 6th March, 1962. *David Dykes*

Coal from Kirkby sidings for Staythorpe power station near Newark climbs past Blidworth & Rainworth on 31st March, 1962 with No. 48317 working hard. *Jack Cupit*

MR-built '4F' class 0-6-0 No. 43870 gets into its stride on the Mid-Notts Joint (Farnsfield-Ollerton) line with coal from Bilsthorpe Colliery to Nottingham. In this 1962 view the train was routed via Kirklington, Southwell and the Rolleston West curve. *J.S. Hancock*

FURTHER GROWTH IN THE COALFIELD, 1930 TO CLOSURE

On 11th April. 1964 '4F' class No. 44213 is helping (or should it be hindering?) an unidentified Stanier '8F' 2-8-0 as they bowl along near Farnsfield with a heavy load of what purports to be coal, but in reality appears to be slack fit only for use at a power station. *J.S. Hancock*

Stanier '8F' class 2-8-0 No. 48102 leads a Brush type 4 diesel (later class '47') in its original two-tone green livery on the climb out of Clipstone Colliery whose spoil heap is prominent in this view. *Booklaw Publications*

Brush type '4' No. D1826 is seen removing stored wagons on 16th October, 1965. The bridge carries the Blidworth Colliery line that was built in the late 1920s. Blidworth Junction signal box is to the left. *J.S. Hancock*

The Railway Enthusiasts Club's 'The Collier No. 2' railtour at Rufford Colliery Junction on 16th March, 1968. The train ran from Nottingham (Midland) and took in a number of freight-only lines in the East Midlands. The lead vehicle is a Cravens driving motor brake second (later class '105'). *J.S. Hancock*

Farnsfield goods shed on 28th December, 1983. As 'The Old Goods Yard' this building has been artfully re-purposed as a six bedroom home on three floors. *J.S. Hancock*

The Southwell Trail

Whilst the remaining section of the line was still operational west of Farnsfield, a scheme was prepared which would give a new life to the use of the trackbed to the east of Farnsfield. Once the track in this section had been removed, Nottinghamshire County Council decided to purchase the trackbed in order to turn it into a public footpath. However it became rather more than that; it became designated as a 'Trail'. The outcome is that it is now possible to walk along the trackbed from Bilsthorpe all the way to Southwell.

The delightful scenery can enable those who walk along it to get a sense of what it might have been like to take this scenic journey by train. Where once there was a station yard at Farnsfield now, at the beginning of the 'Trail', there are car parking facilities and picnic areas have been created. The same facility can be found at Kirklington, which is also in the former station yard. Parking for cars is also provided at Southwell where the 'Trail' ends.

During this period the station buildings on this section were sold off and became private dwellings.

Three views of the Southwell Trail taken near the site of Farnsfield goods yard in February 2021. *David Fudger*

With the town of Mansfield as the backdrop a pair of class '20s' with a brake van prepare to pass under Windsor Road, Mansfield on 8th November, 1978. The ground frame and the siding turnout leading to the Berry Hill Quarry sidings of the Mansfield Standard Sand Co. can be seen in the foreground. Fisher Lane Park is to the right.   *Malcolm Rush*

The same pair of class '20s' pass Berry Hill Quarry Sidings on their way to Mansfield Colliery Junction on 8th November, 1978.   *Malcolm Rush*

FURTHER GROWTH IN THE COALFIELD, 1930 TO CLOSURE

The final years

With the Southwell line truncated it was the Eastern Region which now had the major share of the coal traffic being moved out from this group of collieries.

By May 1975 the overall arrangements were as follows:

Bilsthorpe Colliery, Blidworth Colliery and Mansfield Colliery were 'single serviced' by the Eastern Region.
Rufford Colliery and Clipstone Colliery were 'dual serviced' by the Eastern and London Midland regions.

This resulted in the former Mansfield Railway having the lion's share of the traffic. To give a comparison, the movement of coal at this stage was as follows*

Bilsthorpe	4,000 tons each day using the Eastern Region
Blidworth	2,500 tons each day using the Eastern Region
Mansfield	2,460 tons each day using the Eastern Region
Clipstone	360 tons each day using the Eastern Region
	4,600 tons each day using the London Midland Region line
Rufford	2,100 tons each day using the Eastern Region
	750 tons each day using the London Midland Region line

It will be seen that in total the Eastern Region (the former Mansfield Railway) was moving out 11,420 tons each day compared with 5,350 tons each day on the former LMS (Mansfield-Southwell) line.

No. 20169 at Berry Hill Quarry Sidings with 8T59 (the Metal Box train) on 3rd April, 1979. The engine had previously travelled, with two Railfreight 45 ton 'VCA' vans and a brake van, past Mansfield South Junction to Sherwood Colliery Sidings South where the engine ran round and proceeded back to Mansfield South Junction. It then propelled the train along the branch to the Berry Hill Quarry Sidings. Leaving the two 'VCAs' and brake van on the branch running line. No. 20169 then proceeded into the sidings where three vans were collected (the first of which had just been hand loaded from a lorry with bags of loco sand). The three vans were then attached to some open wagons (seen in this view). The two 'VCAs' and brake van were then collected from the running line and the train proceeded back to Mansfield South Junction and on to Kirkby Summit where it was propelled on the siding leading to the Oddicroft Lane Metal Box factory, Sutton-in-Ashfield. After more shunting the two loaded 'VCA' vans, containing tinplate, were left at the Metal Box plant. *Malcolm Rush*

* Official figures provided by the National Coal Board.

Class '44' 1Co-Co1 No. 44002 (named *Helvellyn* in its earlier days) passes Mansfield Colliery Junction signal box on 3rd June, 1977. Just in view is a class '20'. *J.S. Hancock*

Seen from Oak Tree Lane overbridge, Nos. 20070 and 20196 pass Mansfield Colliery Junction with a coal train, probably from Clipstone Colliery, on 24th March, 1983. *Malcolm Rush*

FURTHER GROWTH IN THE COALFIELD, 1930 TO CLOSURE

Nos. 20178 and 20172 propel a brake van past Mansfield Colliery Junction, heading towards Rufford Colliery Sidings on 24th March, 1983. The engines are passing the advanced up starting signal (No. 14). The lower signal is the down outer home (No. 7). *Malcolm Rush*

Class '20s' Nos. 20164 and 20158 are seen with a loaded train from Clipstone Colliery. The signalman at Rufford Colliery Sidings is exchanging single line authority for the train to proceed to Mansfield Colliery Junction, 17th September, 1979. *Malcolm Rush*

Complete closure

In September 1983 it was decided that the use of the former Mansfield-Southwell line was no longer economical and it was felt that it would be more so for the collieries to be serviced entirely by the former Mansfield Railway. This move brought to an end the former Midland influence and with the closure of this section west of Farnsfield the Mansfield-Southwell line ceased to exist. The track was lifted and eventually some of the trackbed in this section, especially in the area around Rainworth, was later used to effect improvements in the road system with Rainworth being effectively by-passed for those driving to and from the A614.

In conclusion

The Mansfield-Southwell-Rolleston railway certainly had a shaky start with the Midland dragging its heels and a local community showing a fervent determination to have the line built. It could be argued that the original misgivings of the Midland were justified as far as passenger services were concerned as the comparatively early demise of this element seems to indicate. However, in hindsight it is very clear that following the development of the coalfield in the area through which the railway ran and the operation of the line in the movement of coal, ultimately justified building it.

Class '20s' Nos. 20047 and 20178 cross the River Maun as they approach Mansfield South Junction on 28th February, 1983. *Malcolm Rush*

Chapter Five

Motive power

The nature of the line meant that the scope of motive power was somewhat limited. There is no clear indication of the types being used when the line first opened between Rolleston and Southwell.

There is a photograph showing a Midland 4-4-0 taken near Mansfield Colliery Junction in 1905 (when the branch to the colliery opened) and before the signal box was built, but it is not hauling a train (*see page 38*).

Freight trains were in the hands of Samuel W. Johnson/Richard Deeley 0-6-0 tender engines. Some 935 of these engines were built over a 33 year period from 1875, some by the Midland Railway at its works in Derby, but many others by outside constructors. Over the many years of service these locomotives gave (the last member of class in BR service was not withdrawn until 1964) there were numerous variants and rebuilds. Differences included driving wheel diameter, cylinder dimensions, boilers and fireboxes and working pressure. The LMS classified the locomotives working to a boiler pressure of 160 psi as '2F' while those at 175 psi became '3F'.

The first examples of the more powerful Fowler '4F' class 0-6-0s were introduced by the Midland Railway as the '3835' class in 1911. By the time the final batch of '4Fs' was produced, by the LMS in 1941, more than 700 had been constructed. In BR days locomotives Nos. 44414 and 44416 were seen very regularly on the line, much to the bane of junior locospotters!

The motive power needed in the later years was appropriate for the main purpose of the line, mainly for the haulage of coal and to a lesser extent, for a period, the oil trains and those taking sand from the quarries. For the purpose of moving these commodities, the ubiquitous LMS Stanier '8F' class 2-8-0s were very much in evidence. This class was constructed between 1935 and 1946 and eventually totalled more than 800 examples.

Later the Austerity 'WD' class 2-8-0s made an appearance. These locomotives were designed by R.A. Riddles during World War II, with more than 900 of the type constructed by North British Locomotive Co. in Glasgow and the Vulcan Foundry in Newton-le-Willows between 1943 and 1945 for the War Department. Of these, 200 were purchased by the LNER and another 533 were acquired by British Railways in 1948. Ultimately they were numbered in series by BR from '90000'. The 'WDs' were based on the Stanier '8F' design but with significant cost-saving modifications. Key differences between the types were the boiler and firebox, a parallel boiler with round-topped copper steel firebox was used on the 'WD', while Stanier's '8F' had a tapered boiler and a Belpaire copper firebox.

The 'Rolleston Paddy' was, for many years, indeed most of its time, propelled by Midland Railway 0-4-4Ts built to a S.W. Johnson design. In British Railways days Nos. 58085 and 58086, which had been constructed for the Midland Railway by Dübs & Co. of Glasgow in 1900, were regular performers. The 0-4-4Ts were stationed at Southwell engine shed, to the east of Southwell station. It was a sub-shed of Nottingham (Midland). Southwell shed after its official closure on 10th

A rather smoky view of the engine shed at Southwell where 0-4-4T No. 58065 has ventured up to take a drink standing partly over the ash pit. The sub-shed was somewhat generously furnished with two water cranes.
Jack Cupit

Midland Railway 0-4-4T No. 58065, bearing its 36E Newark shedplates, is seen at the former Great Northern engine shed. Gresley 'J6' class 0-6-0s No. 64234 and 64259 keep the push-pull fitted engine company. 'J6s' were occasional visitors to Southwell.
P.H. Groom

Still carrying an LMS number, ex-Midland Railway Johnson '3F' class 0-6-0 No. 3529 is seen on a westbound goods train at Southwell *circa* 1950. *Douglas Thompson*

Hughes/Fowler 'Crab' 2-6-0s were regular performers on excursion trains over the Southwell line. No. 42769 is seen here at Farnsfield on 12th April, 1952. *H.B. Priestley*

Riddles 'Austerity' 'WD' class 2-8-0 No. 90529 is seen passing Mansfield Colliery Junction signal box on 4th September, 1965. *Author*

January, 1955 remained *in situ* until an accident where part of the building was damaged and this led to demolition.

With Southwell shed closed, Newark shed (ex-Great Northern Railway) took on responsibility for locomotive affairs for passenger trains on the Southwell line. This meant that occasionally 'foreign' engines could be found on the local passenger service, although these would not be push-pull fitted. These included ex-Great Northern 'J6' class 0-6-0s and an ex-Great Central Railway Robinson 'A5' class 4-6-2T.

Visiting motive power used latterly to head the Southwell race specials often consisted of locomotives of the Hughes/Fowler '5F' class 2-6-0. These were introduced by the LMS in 1926 and were often referred to as 'Crabs'.

After Mansfield engine shed closed on 11th April, 1960 Kirkby-in-Ashfield became the principal source for motive power for freight workings. By the mid-1960s Kirkby-in-Ashfield engine shed would see English Electric type '1s' (later class '20'), BR type '2s' (later class '25') and Brush type '4s' (later class '47'). The shed at Kirkby-in-Ashfield officially closed to steam in 1966, although some '8Fs' are known to have lingered into 1967. It continued with diesels until final closure in November 1970. From that point onwards the motive power requirements for the Southwell line were fulfilled by locomotives from Toton (Nottingham) depot.

The class '20' 1,000 bhp Bo-Bos dominated the traffic in the line's final years. These locomotives had a cab at one end only, so were often operated running double-headed coupled nose-to-nose. Examples of the type were built for over a decade from 1957 and were eventually to number more than 200 in the class. They gained a reputation for reliability when other classes of diesels were presenting teething troubles on introduction. By the 1970s more than 100 class '20s' were allocated to Toton motive power depot.

The diesel-electric class '25s' 1,250hp were built between 1961 and 1967 and had Sulzer engines. This class eventually totalled more than 300 locomotives. Most were built by BR at Crewe, Darlington and Derby, but some were ordered from Beyer, Peacock in Manchester. By the 1970s around 50 class '25s' were based at Toton.

The class '47' Co-Co, 2,580 bhp from the mid-1960s onwards, was the most numerous and ubiquitous of all main line diesel-electric locomotives in the country with 512 examples. Built by Brush in Loughborough and BR at Crewe, these locomotives had Sulzer engines.

There were ten BR class '44' Sulzer-engined 1Co-Co1s. Classifed as type '4', prior to the introduction of the Total Operations Processing System (TOPS) they had carried the numbers D1-D10, and bore names of mountains, becoming known as 'Peaks'. Originally intended as passenger locomotives, they suffered reliability problems in their early days. They were usurped from passenger duties by the more powerful Sulzer class '45s' and '46s' (also known as 'Peaks'). The steam heating boilers were removed from the class '44s' and the entire class was then allocated to Toton and employed on freight work including on the Southwell line. They were withdrawn from service between 1976 and 1980.

In 1982, the class '45' 'Peaks', were in turn usurped from Midland main line passenger duties, by the arrival of High Speed Train (HST) multiple units, and subsequently demoted to secondary duties, including on the Southwell line.

Motive power variety at Mansfield Colliery Junction as a Stanier '8F' class 2-8-0 is piloting a BR type '2' (later class '25'). In the foreground is Riddles 'Austerity' 'WD' class 2-8-0 No. 90529. *Author*

Brush type '4' (later class '47') Co-Co No. D1816 with a westbound coal train passing Mansfield Colliery Junction signal box on 15th June, 1965. *J.S. Hancock*

Class '44' 1Co-Co1 No. 44004 draws its train of loaded coal wagons into the shunting spur at Mansfield Colliery Junction on 17th September, 1979. The train was from Rufford Colliery and was bound for Avenue Sidings. However, No. 44004 (the erstwhile *Great Gable*) was suffering from a lack of engine power so the wagons were shunted into the sidings seen on the left. *Malcolm Rush*

Sources

The House of Lords Record Office

Copies of Acts of Parliament

1846	16th July	9 & 10	Vict.	cap. clvii
1865	5th July	28 & 29	Vict.	cap. ccclix
1869	12th July	32 & 33	Vict.	cap. lxxxiii
1926	30th June	16 & 17	Geo. 5	ch. xxxii
1926	15th July	16 & 17	Geo. 5	ch. xlv

Railway timetables – Midland, LMS and BR

Newspaper reports

Nottingham Journal
Nottingham Evening Post
Mansfield Reporter
Stamford Mercury
Sheffield Daily Telegraph
Sheffield Independent
Derbyshire Times
Derbyshire Courier

London Sporting Chronicle
Yorkshire Post
The Scotsman
Birmingham Daily Gazette
Rugby Advertiser
Nottinghamshire &
  Midland Counties Daily Express

and others (mainly consulted through the National Newspaper Archive).

The John Swift Collection, copyright the Signalling Record Society.

Acknowledgements and thanks

My thanks to those whose help and advice has been greatly appreciated:

- Russell Rollings for advice and his meticulous proof reading at various stages.
- Bill Taylor for providing various leads and information and also sourcing many photographs.
- J.S. Hancock for the use of his photographs.
- Malcolm Rush for providing photographs and captions.
- John Hitchens for loaning material from his extensive collection of railway reports and documents.
- David Fudger for photographs of the Southell Trail.
- Jim Jackson, a former fireman based at Southwell.
- I am also very grateful to the staff of the House of Lords Record Office who located a number of Acts of Parliament relating to the line.
- Many thanks also to Ian Kennedy (with whom I have worked for many years) for turning the various elements into a book.

Index

Accidents and incidents, 24, 32, 39, 109
Acts of Parliament, 7, 8, 14, 15, 21 et seq., 48
Barrow, W.P., MP, 20
Berry Hill Sand Co., 29
Bilsthorpe Colliery, 50, 51, 62, 63, 69, 101
Blidworth Colliery and branch, 29, 41, 47, 48, 51, 58 et seq., 101
Blidworth & Rainworth, 28, 29, 32, 45, 47, 54, 68, 93
Board of Trade inspection, 25
Bolsover Colliery Co., 37, 39
British Railways, 65, 67, 77, 93, 101
Bus services, 12, 49, 51, 52
Clay Cross & Newark Railway, 6, 7 et seq.
Clipstone Colliery, 39, 48, 59, 93, 101
Closure to goods, 93, 104
Closure to passengers,
  Mansfield to Southwell, 52
  Southwell to Rolleston Junction, 77
Coal traffic, 37 et seq., 50 et seq., 58 et seq., 93, 101, 105
Crown Farm Colliery
  (see Mansfield Colliery)
D'Arcy Exploration Co., 65
Denison, Rt Hon. J.E., 12, 18
Duke of Portland, 47
Eckersley & Bayliss, 23, 25
Elmsley level crossing, 62
Excursions, 13, 33, 51, 54, 77, 82, 83
Farnsfield, 10, 25, 29, 33, 34, 45, 48, 50 et seq., 54, 59, 62, 68, 93, 99
Fiskerton, 9, 11, 12
Great Northern Railway, 20, 21, 33
Grouping, 39
Handyside & Co., 23
Hemingway & Co., 37
Hexgreave Estates, 51
Hodgkinson, Mr, MP, 17, 18
Hollins, William, 12, 21
Hudson, George, 6, 18, 21
Kirkby-in-Ashfield, 37, 52, 109
Kirklington & Edingley, 25, 29, 30, 36, 45, 51, 52, 55, 62, 69, 93, 99
Locomotives, 105 et seq.
Logan & Hemingway, 47
London Midland & Scottish Rly, 33, 39, 41, 47, 48, 50 et seq., 58, 59, 62
London & North Eastern Railway, 39, 41, 47, 48, 50, 51
London & North Western Railway, 13, 23, 24
Mansfield & District Tramways, 49

Mansfield Colliery, 37, 41, 43, 52, 54, 58, 59, 101
Mansfield Colliery Junction, 39, 43, 58, 59, 67
Mansfield East Junction, 42, 67
Mansfield engine shed, 42, 105, 109
Mansfield North Junction, 42, 66
Mansfield Railway, 37, 39, 41, 50, 101, 104
Mansfield Sand Co., 29, 39, 47
Mansfield South Junction, 42, 66
Mansfield (Town) station, 42, 66, 77, 85
Midland Railway, 6, 7 et seq., 13, 15 et seq., 39
Mid-Nottinghamshire Joint Railway, 48 et seq., 61, 65, 96
Millward, R., 17 et seq.
National Coal Board, 65
Newark Corporation Waterworks siding, 54, 62
Newark engine shed, 77, 109
Newstead Colliery Co., 41, 47, 51
Nottingham-Lincoln line (MR), 7, 25, 52, 55
Oil traffic, 63, 65, 105
Ollerton, 48, 49, 51
Opening of the line,
  Rolleston to Southwell, 9
  Southwell to Mansfield, 25, 29
'The Paddy', 52, 62, 65, 77 et seq., 105
Rainworth, see Blidworth & Rainworth
Rolleston Junction, 46
Rolleston south curve, 52, 55
Rolleston West, 52, 71
Rufford Colliery and branch, 39, 41, 44, 47, 48, 52, 54, 59, 68, 93, 101
Sand traffic, 29, 39, 47, 54, 58, 76, 105
Settle & Carlisle Railway, 18, 23, 24
Signalling, 25, 39, 41, 58, 59, 62, 66 et seq.
Southwell, 7, 25, 46, 55, 71
Southwell engine shed, 25, 55, 109
Southwell racecourse, 33, 53, 54, 77, 83, 109
Southwell Trail, 99
Stanton Ironworks Co., 50
Stenton, Mr, 19, 20
Stephenson & Co., 9, 10
Timetables, 9 et seq., 16, 29, 31 et seq., 35, 36, 50, 62 et seq., 72 et seq.
Upton Crossing, 52, 71
Walker, Sir E.S., 12
World War I, 37, 63
World War II, 62, 63